The Pearl *of* Congo

The incredible *true story* of one woman's journey of
love and sacrifice for the orphaned children of Congo

TEDDY M. CLARK

The Pearl of Congo

Trilogy Christian Publishers A Wholly Owned Subsidiary of Trinity Broadcasting Network

2442 Michelle Drive Tustin, CA 92780

Cover design by: Kelly Stewart

For information about special discounts for bulk purchases, please contact Trilogy Christian Publishing.

Manufactured in the United States of America

10 9 8 7 6 5 4 3 2 1

Library of Congress Cataloging-in-Publication Data is available.

ISBN: 978-1-68556-038-6

E-ISBN: 978-1-68556-039-3

DEDICATION

To my loving mother, Mae Pearl Clark, who dedicated her entire life to loving and serving unwanted children.

To my wife, Evelyn, who's been supportive throughout this entire journey and without whose help I could not have written this book.

And to my orphan brothers and sisters who died in the Congo.

"Every joy, every trial, every heartache that the Lord has led me to has made me richer and deeper in love with Him."

— MAE PEARL CLARK

ACKNOWLEDGMENTS

I want to thank my family and friends that contributed information for the book, including my mom, Mae Pearl Clark, and some of the orphan children. Mr. and Mrs. Ed and Taylora Dial, for giving me the idea to write this book and encouraging me throughout the process, and Timothy Lind, who also contributed information for this book.

CONTENTS

ENDORSEMENTS

The Pearl of Congo is an inspiring story of one woman's faith, compassion, and perseverance. It provides a look into the life of missionary Mae Clark and includes some interesting world history from her perspective. Mae's love for God and willingness to go wherever He sent her allowed her to impact the lives of many children. I appreciate the inclusion of both her triumphs and disappointments, as it makes her that much more relatable. Mae never lost hope and relied on God's provision throughout her life. The fact this book was written by one of her children demonstrates how much she was loved and the impact her life had. This story encourages, instills hope, and reminds us of the importance of human connection and kindness.

KRISTIN L. GRAY
Psy.D.

—

Inspirational and empowering! Amazing how one woman determined to do God's work found all the courage she needed through faith and the power of prayer. Mae is a great Christian role model. The children she saved and the determination she had is remarkable. This book left me feeling hopeful and inspired and renewed my faith in the power of prayer.

TRACI YORK
Correctional Counselor II, Department of Corrections

—

I could not put the book down. What an amazing documentary about a true dedicated, sacrificial, selfless, and loving soul. Mae's life made me reevaluate my relationship with God and my walk with God. This documentary of Mae's life, makes me want to be a much better person (caused me to repent) and a much better submitted servant because of the example of true love Mae displayed in difficult and heart wrenching circumstances. She was steadfast and she kept the faith! I never personally met Mae, but I love her, and I now understand why Teddy's character and behavior is so above his peers. Not with arrogance or pride or disdain, but so even tempered with the same love, commitment and faithfulness to God, just like his beautiful and esteemed mother. With all love, respect and believing that you will continue to have much success in life. This book is a great read about a very gracious and courageous person.

JEFFREY G. TAYLOR
CEO, Fortitude Power Inc.

—

In my opinion every young person should read this book. Also if someone thinks they're having a difficult life, this is a must read for them, [it is] an exceptional testimony.

MARY D. MOPPINS
Warden, Department of Corrections

—

An incredible story of a tenacious woman of faith! A true testament to the power of prayer, God's provision and his unconditional love through the heart of Mae. A story that transports us across significant historical moments where the hand of God is evident in every moment and the fruit of his works are evident in the lives of the children she touched!

A must read! A true depiction of carrying out God's calling from the start of Mae's journey with God to the writing of this book.

SHARON MORENO
M.A, Psychology, Social Worker

—

Resilient! Many times Mae Clark was unsure of what to do or lacked the resources to do them but that never swayed her. In her mind, she was a full-time employee of the Lord. So if something was a problem, the solution was prayer. Few of us have Mae's unwavering faith, reading this story will encourage you to go deeper in your relationship with the Lord.

RICHARD KOON
VP Ministry Lending, America's Christian Credit Union

"God had an only Son
and He made him a missionary".

— DAVID LIVINGSTONE

PREFACE

As I write this, I still don't feel fully adequate or prepared to do so. If I had waited to feel ready to write my mother's story, I would have never written it. I pray this story inspires you to step out into what God has called you to do despite any fears, lack of answers, or even lack of faith. You might not know the whole plan, and it might not even make sense, but it's an opportunity to see God do the impossible.

There are guaranteed roadblocks that will make you want to quit or make you doubt who He is or who you are or both. My hope is that my mother's story will remind you to keep going; God will open doors and reveal His grace and strength during the journey and not before. When you encounter a wall, don't give in, don't give up because anything worthwhile takes hard work, resilience, and faith.

"Let us not become weary in doing good,
for at the proper time we will reap
a harvest if we do not give up."

GALATIANS 6:9

INTRODUCTION

One early morning, on January 25th, 1964, two armed rebel soldiers approached the compound. They arrived at Mae's doorstep and knocked on the door. They asked Mae if there were any national soldiers on the compound. Mae answered *"No, only children."* In spite of her response, they went through the compound, area by area, checking carefully for hidden soldiers. While inside the orphanage, they grabbed food and other items and then went on their way. The next day, there was another knock on the door. When Mae answered the door, the rebel soldier, who described himself as "Kosantine," put a gun to her head and this time didn't ask but told her to tell him where the military soldiers were hiding. He told her that there were twenty-five rebel soldiers surrounding the orphanage compound, so she'd better tell the truth. Mae assured him again that there were no military soldiers around. He didn't believe her, so he told Mae that he and his men would remain in the compound for an undetermined amount of time until the soldiers were found.

The next day, the village chief heard about

what was happening in the compound. He decided to go to the compound and explain to the soldier in charge who Mae was and what contributions she was making to the orphanage and village. He didn't find the soldier in charge, so he told the soldier to pass on this information to the rebel leader, who was named Pierre Mulele. The soldier said he would. The next day, the soldier brought back a message to Mae and told her that no harm would come to her as long as no national soldiers were allowed on the compound or were in communication with her. However, if she didn't comply, her life would be in jeopardy. The rebel soldiers were posted in the area around the compound from that day on.

The United Nations was aware that Mae's orphanage now resided in a rebel-occupied zone. A few weeks later, officials decided that Mae needed to abandon the area for her own safety. The UN, then, sent a plane that flew over the compound and dropped numerous notes notifying Mae of the attempted rescue. The rescue involved a helicopter for the very next day. The rescue would be for only her as an American citizen, but, unfortunately, the Congolese orphan children would have to stay.

The rebels saw the plane dropping notes over the orphanage and came to Mae and threatened her life again since they thought she was selling them out to the military somehow. Mae was able to convince the rebel soldiers that she would never put the children's lives in jeopardy for any reason. The soldiers said they would be prepared to fight if anything wrong were to happen.

Unfortunately, the weather did not permit the rescue to take place the following day. A few days later, the plane once again flew over, and a note was dropped for a next-day rescue, the same as before. In the note, Mae was instructed to be in the open field of the compound, standing alone on top of white sheets on the ground, so she could be seen from above, waiting for the rescue. The next morning, Mae did as instructed. The helicopters came but did not land because they did not see Mae anywhere, so they returned to the capital. Mae wasn't sure what had happened. There was high grass all around in the open field, and so Mae assumed they just didn't see her. After a few days, the plane flew over again, dropping more notes stating there would be another rescue attempt the next day. Mae thought that this time had to be it! So, the next morning, she said goodbye to the children and assured them it wouldn't be long until they were rescued too.

Two planes and four helicopters came to rescue Mae, but only two of the helicopters landed. When they landed, armed UN soldiers came out of one helicopter with guns drawn and told Mae to get in the other helicopter. Mae did as she was told, and she got in. As she was being airlifted back to the capital city of Leopoldville, she asked why the children couldn't have been rescued with her. They told her that the orders were to only rescue her and that she would have to take the rest of the matter up with the top UN officials or the prime minister. Mae was devastated and relieved all at the same time.

THE BEGINNING

Mae Pearl Clark was born to Joseph and Anne Clark on February 17th, 1910, the same date her mother was born, twenty-nine years earlier. Her dad, Joseph, was born on September 6th, 1879. Mae was born in a small, rural town outside of Baltimore, Maryland. When she was a toddler, Mae's family moved to Meyersdale, Pennsylvania, where they lived on a farm. Mae grew up the third youngest of seven children. She had three sisters: Alice, the oldest; Alma, the youngest; and an older sister named Clara. She also had three brothers: George, Elmer, and Earl. Her mom and dad worked tirelessly on the farm since that was their livelihood. Mae learned hard work as a child. Growing up, Mae and her siblings had to wake up at four in the morning to do their chores before going to school.

When Mae was eight years old, the US got involved in World War I, otherwise known as "The Great War." The government encouraged the country to contribute to the war's cause by buying war bonds along with other resources. All Americans of all ages were encouraged to get involved and help. Mae's family were small-town farmers, but Mae and her siblings would contribute by growing food in the garden for the troops overseas. Mae also participated when local schools got involved by growing gardens and writing and sending letters to the troops overseas. Her dad left home to help with the cause of the war, and she and her siblings had to pick up the load in his absence. The work on the farm doubled, and they continued to work early in the morning and after school. Mae's dad returned from time to time and also did mining work when there was work available. The family was always concerned for his safety since fatalities were common in the mines. It was a very dangerous and physically challenging job, and he would continue working for Union Mining throughout his career. From the age of five to fourteen, Mae would continue working on the farm while going to school. After eighth grade, Mae's parents decided that she had to drop out of school to work full time on the farm. That was the extent of her formal education.

Mae and her family did not grow up religious people, nor did they attend church, but she began attending a small church a walking distance from her house when she was about eighteen years old. After attending church for a few months, she accepted Jesus Christ as her personal Lord and Savior. One Sunday, a few months later, Mae met a young lady, who was a couple of years older, named Marie Forsberg. She had also come to know the Lord through the church a year or so earlier. They hit it off right away and became good friends. Their relationship over time would grow, and they would eventually become best friends. Mae was excited about God and told her family about it, but her family was not too receptive to her new religion. After a year of attending the church, the pastor one day talked about how young adults were needed in ministry to work in a small town in Royalton, Kentucky, near the Appalachian Mountains. At nineteen years of age, Mae thought about this opportunity. However, it involved making a big decision that would take her life on a completely different course than she had planned. Mae told the pastor that she would go. She wondered what it would mean to work full-time for the Lord. She went home and told her family about her desire, but she knew that they would not want her to go so far away.

As she had expected, her family did not approve of her going and told her that she was needed at home. Mae thought that her parents' request was more about them being protective because of her health. While growing up, Mae had been sick a lot more than her siblings. It would be easier on her parents if Mae stayed close to home. Mae wasn't sure what to do, but after a few weeks, the decision was made for her. There was talk everywhere about the country being in a depression, with banks closing and lots of people being out of work everywhere. The year was 1929. Mae realized this wasn't the right time to leave home. She knew she would be needed at home now more than ever. Mae told the pastor that she had changed her mind, not knowing if the opportunity would still be available in the future. The pastor was disappointed but understood why Mae had changed her mind. Mae stayed home a few more years in order to help her family try to survive the challenges that lay ahead of them. The depression would be a difficult time for Mae and her family. The depression did not just impact the US; it was felt around the world. Mae's family would work hard on the farm just to keep from losing it. The first few years were the most difficult. Thankfully, they did not end up losing their farm, and after a few years, things seemed to be stable—although the depression would last for much longer.

Mae's heart and mind still felt the tug to go to Royalton for full-time ministry. So she discussed these things with her best friend Marie, and Marie told her that she wanted to go also. Marie thought they should both go since there was a continual need, and it was still on both their hearts to do so. Mae asked the pastor yet again if there was still a need and if there were openings to go to the Appalachian Mountains. The pastor said yes and was delighted that she was still willing to go after several years had passed since she first spoke to him about it. Mae let her family know, once again, about what she wanted to do, although not much had changed in the economy. However, she felt she had contributed enough to her family, and it was time to move on. Mae and Marie waited another year before leaving Pennsylvania to go to Kentucky to serve the Lord. Their home church right outside of Meyersdale gave their blessings and sent Mae and Marie off to work in the Appalachian Mountains. Although the depression was still going on in the country, it seemed like President Roosevelt was making better progress with his new programs, which ultimately put more people to work around the country.

Mae Pearl Clark in 1929,
a year after she accepted Christ

THE GROUNDWORK

By the fall of 1934, the country was hoping that the worst of the depression was behind them. Some jobs were opening up, and things looked a little bit better. Mae left home since her family was better prepared, although they still did not fully understand why she wanted to leave for religious, full-time work. Mae did not let her family's disapproval stop her from getting to Kentucky. She left by bus after saying goodbye to her family in Meyersdale. God was her employer now, whether she got paid a little or a lot. Mae and Marie arrived in Royalton, Kentucky, in 1934, not knowing what to expect. They didn't know where they would live or how much money they would make, but they were comforted by knowing they were obeying what God had placed in both their hearts.

When they arrived in Royalton, they met a nice couple, Mr. and Mrs. Gary, who was waiting for them at the train station. The couple was very nice to them and overall very helpful. They took Mae and Marie to lunch and to the small place where they would reside. The place was a small cabin that consisted of one bedroom, a living room, and a small kitchen that had an oil stove. Right outside the house was an outhouse. It was an old house with no electricity, and the bedroom had two cots to sleep on. Since the cabin had no electricity, it was nice that there was a fireplace since it would be much needed on cold nights. There was also an extra small room for storage, which they named the "Rat Room" since that's where everything landed— all their lesson plans, books, papers, curriculum, etc. They would have to save up to buy a wood stove. Friends loaned them some pots and pans, so they at least had something to cook in. It was enough to get started for what they needed.

The next morning, Mae and Marie were given a tour of the town by Mr. and Mrs. Gary, and it only took them a couple of hours to see everything since it was a small town. Mae and Marie had to go into town in order to get their water. They had to use the town pump and carry it back to their home. The town was nestled between hills, and a railroad went right through it, with houses on each side of the railroad track. Down at the end of the town was the railroad station and a general store, mostly used by the folks that lived in town. On the right side of the tracks, right against the hill, was the school.

Mae and Marie lived about a mile and a half from the school. When it snowed, they would have to dig out the snow path to get to the coals outside. They had to bring them back for the fireplace in order to keep warm, and they used candles for lights since there wasn't electricity.

They struggled the first few months, with barely enough food to eat each day. They would pray for food in the morning during their daily devotional and again at the end of the day. Mae said sometimes it felt like the heavens were made of grass, and their prayers were not going any higher than the ceiling. It felt as if God was not answering their prayers. One particular morning, Mae and Marie were about to make breakfast when they realized they had run out of food. To make matters worse, they did not have any money to go buy food, so they decided to pray. When they finished, there was a knock on the door. At the door was a lady who said she was a neighbor from down the road, and she was holding a full, big bag of green beans. She said she felt led to share some green beans with "The Girls." From then on, Mae and Marie would be known around town as "The Girls." Marie gladly accepted the bag of green beans from her neighbor and thanked the Lord for them. They had beans to last them a few days. Mae and Marie rejoiced and praised God for His provision.

Still, after several months of living there, they realized that it would be difficult to come up with the rent money every month. To make matters worse, the manager was a mean, grouchy, and intimidating man. He cursed like a sailor and smoked like a train. They knew he was not a religious man at all. They tried not to wait until the last minute to pay their rent, but sometimes they didn't come up with the money until the very last day of the month.

The manager would tell them, *"Good thing you made it on time; I was beginning to think I would have to throw you out."* On one occasion, they had asked the manager if he could wait for a little longer, not knowing if they would have it by the end of the week. And, as before, he threatened to throw them out. They got on their knees and prayed for God to provide the rent money. They prayed to the Lord, *"We don't believe You brought us here just to get kicked out." We believe You will provide for us; although we have no idea where it's going to come from, we will put our trust in You."*

That evening, as they were eating dinner, there was a knock on the door. Mae opened the door, and an older lady said, *"Hi, girls,"* with a big smile on her face. She was a friend from their church, whom they had led to Christ. The lady mentioned that her husband had just recently been saved. She said that the family had been talking about tithes and offerings, and they had prayed last night and felt the Lord telling them to give them an offering. Mae and Marie began to cry while praising God. Mae, with tears in her eyes, explained their situation to her, and the lady then began to cry also. She was so shocked and humbled that the Lord would use her family in that capacity to be an immediate blessing by being obedient and bringing the four dollars from their family to give to Mae and Marie. That evening, they gave thanks again to God for not forgetting about their needs. At that moment, Mae felt in her spirit that Royalton was a training ground for something bigger to come. She wasn't sure what, but she knew it was something!

The weather was extreme at times, and winters were often very cold. Their first few winters, they would experience lots of snow, so much so that they had to dig their way out to get to the outhouse.

Mae recalled her first winter in Royalton, where they found themselves short of coal and short on money. They needed the warmth of the stove, but coal was expensive. They were desperate and had prayed all week because they knew it was only a matter of days before they ran out of coal. That cold December day came, and they only had a few cents between them. They knew they didn't have enough money to buy coal. Temperatures reached zero degrees that night, and they prayed as they had done so before when they needed something.

The next morning, there was a knock on the door. Mae opened the door, and there stood a tall stranger. He asked, *"Ma'am, do you need any coal today?"* Mae and Marie answered, *"Yes, we ran out of coal last night, but we don't have but a couple of cents to pay you."* The man said that he was hoping to sell some coal in exchange for money since his family needed it, but he was willing to give it to them right there. He also mentioned that if they ran out, he had plenty more at the house. Mae felt led to tell the man to come back later that afternoon or the next morning if that was possible. The man agreed, and Mae and Marie gave thanks over the little coal that they had for that cold night.

Shortly after, that same day, Marie felt a need to go to the little store down the street, but she didn't know why. Marie bundled up for the cold, but, thankfully, there was a break in the weather and not too much snow on the ground. When she got to the store, she wondered what to do next since she didn't know why she was there in the first place.

She waited about fifteen minutes, and then the postman arrived. The store owner stated to Marie that it appeared that she had timed things just right, waiting for the break in the weather to walk down here. He then told her that he had mail for her and that if she had come a little earlier, she would have missed it! The store owner gave Marie her mail. The weather appeared to be getting worse, so Marie decided that she'd better go back before it got any worse. When Marie got back, she told Mae she had gone down to the store for some exercise and had picked up a couple of letters in the process. They decided to open the letters before they started doing other things around the house. Marie, all of a sudden, shouted, *"Thank you, Lord!"* Apparently, a relative had sent her some money to help them out. Marie said that this would be enough to cover the coal they had just received.

They praised and thanked God for providing for them. Mae and Marie decided to tithe a tenth of the money that they received, which is what they had always done when they had received money from work or donations. They also felt a burden for the tall gentleman that had knocked on the door since he was desperate for money for his family, but they didn't know why. They prayed that the Lord would also come through for that gentleman who had helped them.

Later in the afternoon, the man came back and brought more coal with him. Mae and Marie were pleasantly surprised to see that after they separated the tithe, they still had enough money left to give the man for the remainder of the coal that he brought. The man would wind up bringing them enough coal to last the entire winter. He told Mae and Marie that they were a new family that recently moved to Royalton, not too far from where Mae and Marie lived. He had a sick young boy, who needed doctor's care, and all he had was coal at his house to exchange for money. They prayed for him and his household right then and there.

Mae and Marie would experience many more stories like that! Since money was always tight, to help with expenses, they would take on extra cleanup work around the school cafeteria by cooking and cleaning when possible! The church was in the same location as the school, so they would have church service there on Sundays. They taught Sunday school to children ages six to eighteen. On Saturdays, the children would come to their home so they could hear more about God. After some of the children were saved, they were excited to bring other friends to the house so Mae and Marie could share the Gospel with them. Mae would also invite the children over on Saturday for Bible study and Bible camps in the summertime when school was out.

The camps and classes began to grow with more children. They worked long hours, but it was rewarding for them because they loved the children. They also visited homes in the town to spread the good news of God's Word. Within a few years, Marie and Mae moved to a four-bedroom townhouse that they shared with two other women. Each of them had their own room, which was a nice change. In just a few years, the town began to grow in population, along with the schools and camps. Mae and Marie would also go to other schools nearby to teach God's Word. Royalton was becoming more than just a small railroad town nestled between hills.

Mae with some of the girls that were at the Bible camp one summer; Boys also attended the camp

Mae and Marie learned to love Kentucky—the hard work, fresh air, and open green spaces, with hills and mountains all around them. The people were proud of their state and heritage. Mae would hear stories of early frontiersmen like Daniel Boone, who apparently was a Bible-believing,

God-fearing Christian who settled his family in Kentucky in the late 1700s. He was also credited for bringing his friends to Kentucky, including the grandparents of Abraham Lincoln, who were also known as God-fearing Christians. Mae and Marie took to the people of Royalton, and the people also took to "The Girls." Even though Mae and Marie were best friends, they also had other friends that they enjoyed being with. Wilma Linkie and Ruth Barrack were two of those friends that they would know throughout the years. The girls' personalities attracted all kinds of people. Mae, especially, was very outgoing and full of life.

On one occasion, Mae was asked out and courted by a young gentleman suitor. He took a fancy to her, and she, in return, took a liking to him. His name was Greg, and he was a Christian who also wanted to be involved in ministry while serving in the military. They courted for a short period of time. One day, Greg was shipped out and stationed a long-distance away, which separated them. After a period of time, Mae stopped hearing from Greg and wondered what had happened to him. She thought that something awful must have happened and was worried sick. She continued to hope and believe that she would hear from him, but she did not. One day, she heard that he was back in town, and she was so shocked that she did not believe it. Marie told her that it was true because she had seen him with someone else. Marie said he told her he was too embarrassed and fearful of breaking the relationship off with her. Mae was hurt and disappointed for a while by the bad news. She saw him in passing every now and then, but after some time, things got back to normal, and she went back to her routine. There was still a lot of work to be done and a bright future to look forward to for Mae.

Mae would remain very busy in the Appalachian Mountains, and soon, weeks turned into months, and months turned into years. She enjoyed the work she was doing and felt it was very rewarding. Throughout the years to come, while at Royalton, she would periodically go back to Pennsylvania and Maryland to visit her family and relatives. When she visited the family, sometimes there were picnics that included sack races for the kids and softball games with the adults. Her brothers and sisters were getting married and having kids, so she tried to stay in touch to see what new things were going on.

Mae was close to her parents and with her brothers and sisters, but she always went back to Royalton because she loved the children, the friendships, and the ministry that went along with it all. Six years had passed since she had been in Royalton.

THE CALL

Mae and Marie had been attending the church
in Royalton for some time when, in the fall of
1940, a special guest speaker came to the church for
a week of revival. On the second night, the preacher
brought up Africa and the need for missionaries
to serve in the Congo. He mentioned that if the
Lord put a desire for missionary work in the heart
of anyone, they should take heed to the calling and
be obedient and respond. Mae heard what he was
saying but didn't pay too close attention to it. The
next evening, the evangelist mentioned it again, and
this time, Mae felt a tug in her heart similarly like
she had before. That evening when she got home,
the pull felt even stronger in her heart, and she
asked, *"Lord, are you calling me for missionary work
in the Congo?"* She prayed about it that evening but
didn't say a word to Marie about it.

The next evening, after the crusade had
finished, she decided to tell Marie about the desire
that was on her heart. When she mentioned it to
Marie, Marie also stated that she felt the same
strong desire. They prayed on it, and on the last
night of the crusade, they told the guest speaker

about their desire to answer the call for the Congo. They told their friends and ministry workers, who were also excited for them. Mae pondered, at night, on how things could change so fast, as she thought with excitement about what the future held for her and her best friend, Marie. She also believed that all things work together for the best. The fact that they were both single and that past relationships hadn't worked out made the decision even easier. Mae thought to herself about her and Marie's close friendship, the struggles and experiences they had shared, and how it seemed their lives were committed to doing the Lord's work wherever He would send them. Mae decided that she would take some time and talk to her family in person about what had just transpired. She went to see them and her family was again very puzzled and didn't understand her decision. They tried to discourage her from going, telling her it was one thing to work in Kentucky for religious reasons, but Africa was dangerous, and it was foolish to go. Especially so for two women who knew nothing about it.

Mae understood her family's concern, but she was not deterred by their comments and returned back to Royalton to prepare for the Congo. They estimated it would take about a year to save and prepare. Mae and Marie began planning for the Congo and thought about how it would affect them psychologically and emotionally to be away from the family. They also thought about the financial uncertainty of not knowing what lay ahead for them or for how long. They continued with their same busy schedule, fulfilling all the obligations their work demanded. They still had bills to pay along with saving up for the big trip ahead. Not to mention, go through the interview and approval process with the missionary board. The director at Royalton told Mae and Marie that they might have a difficult time leaving the States because of the war going on in Europe. He told them that many men and boys, all over the country, had been signing up to enlist in the civil service that year because of the military draft in October of 1940, which included young men twenty-one years old and older. It seemed like the president was taking steps in preparing the country just in case America had to defend itself in a time of war.

Mae and Marie had some boys that came through their camp at Royalton, who joined the military and were now stationed at Pearl Harbor and were aware of the war that was taking place in Europe. It was horrible what Adolf Hitler and his military in Germany were doing to the countries around them. Mae and Marie would pray for all those being killed along with their family and the survivors. It was a scary time for everyone, knowing that one ruthless dictator was trying to conquer other people, causing death and destruction. Despite all this, they felt that until the Lord told them differently, they would continue their pursuit for the Congo. Mae was hopeful that the war would not interfere with her and Marie's plans for going to the Congo.

As time passed, it seemed impossible to come up with the finances for the trip. They could not get the support they needed. The country was still in a depression, so people didn't have any extra funds to support their mission. Mae began to question if God really wanted them to go to the Congo. Maybe it just wasn't meant to be. In 1941, despite their lack of faith, a cousin of Mae's, who lived in Akron, Ohio, who had heard about her situation, wrote her a letter. In the letter, she told Mae that her church had prayed and had decided to sponsor her and Marie for missionary work in the Congo.

THE DELAY

US citizens were strongly advised not to travel outside the country because of the war going on in Europe that had begun a couple of years before. Mae and Marie were not discouraged, primarily because the US and the Congo were not involved in it. They spoke with the state department but could not make any progress. They had worked in Royalton for seven years now and had helped raise the youth in the schools and camps and watched them grow up into productive young men and women. In late 1941, they heard the news that Pearl Harbor was attacked and that the US was now involved in the war. They were devastated. They recalled two boys and one girl in particular, who was a nurse stationed on the base in Hawaii, and they were concerned for their safety and well-being. They anxiously awaited news on whether or not they were still alive. Sometime after, it was confirmed by the parents that the two boys, now men, had been killed at Pearl Harbor. They received news from the nurse, who confirmed the death of the boys but stated that she was safe. Mae and Marie were happy that she had survived but saddened for the two boys and their families. They would mourn their deaths as the rest of the country mourned for their own loved ones who died at Pearl Harbor.

In the summer of 1942, because of Pearl Harbor, there was now another military draft. This time, it included young boys eighteen years old and older. Mae knew some of the families that had to send their boys to war, and even though the boys showed bravery, she knew that their mothers, especially, were fearful for their boys. They knew that letters from the soldiers overseas would mean everything to their families at home, especially to their mothers. This was a difficult period for Mae and Marie as well as the rest of the country. They received confirmation that there was a definite halt on any traveling, with the exception of military personnel. Mae would have to wait until the end of World War II before she could even think about leaving for the Congo.

After Pearl Harbor and the US involvement in the war, Mae and Marie put the Congo on indefinite hold. What did the Lord have for them now? Everything was up in the air; nothing was certain now. No matter what happened, they would

hold on to their belief that God was still in control.
They still put their trust in the Lord and had hope
for the future. As they continued to think and pray
on these things, they also continued to prepare for
the trip financially and spiritually. If ever there was
a time for prayer, it was now.

Mae and Marie in the 1940s
during the war

Throughout the war, Mae would listen to the radio, when possible, to know what was going on. The war would, unfortunately, last longer than anybody ever anticipated. Prayer and work occupied her time, along with other projects that contributed to the war efforts for the next few years. Keeping busy helped her anxiety about the prolonging of missionary work in the Congo. During this time, Mae also had a chance to spend more time with her family back home, and eventually, her parents and family would come to know the Lord. Mae was delighted to know that her family now knew the Lord, and this also brought peace to her heart.

The last few years in Royalton, Kentucky, were just as challenging as the first few. The United States was still at war, and each individual in town would contribute and sacrifice by doing their part. Some bought US savings bonds or war bonds, and for those that could not, they contributed by giving rubber material such as tires. Others took part in the fighting spirit of the nation by singing patriotic songs at church and in the community, such as "Onward Christian Soldier." During this time, Mae and Marie also became good friends with their other two roommates, Wilma Linkie and Ruth

Barrack. As usual, finances were still low, but they tried to save up for the trip to the Congo while meeting the financial needs of everyday life. Some jobs opened up all over the country, not only in factories for war production but other civilian jobs.

Marie had a relative that lived in New York, who told them about part-time jobs during the holiday season. In the wintertime, especially during the holidays, Mae and Marie would travel to New York for work. Mae worked at Macy's and Marie at Woolworths. Marie's cousin offered her home whenever they would go to New York. Because they were seasonal jobs, Mae and Marie could make some extra income since the Bible camps were closed during the holiday season. In January, after the holidays were over, they would go back to Royalton to teach at the school. The seasonal jobs served them well, and it gave them the opportunity to share the Gospel with others, also. They were in constant prayer for all the soldiers fighting overseas, along with those contributing to the war effort at home. They listened on their radio at home to President Roosevelt speak on the war, in what was called "The fireside chats." These "fireside chats" would keep the country abreast of what was happening in each step of the war, from 1941 until the end of the war. Mae and Marie also appreciated the speeches because the president would acknowledge God each time he spoke. The next few years would keep them busy with ministries, jobs, and projects.

Finally, in August of 1945, Mae and Marie heard that the war was finally over. It was almost hard to believe since it seemed like it would never end. There was joy and celebration everywhere. Within the next month, they were summoned to go to Philadelphia to determine if the missionary board members would approve them to travel and do work in the Congo. When they arrived in Philadelphia, they were interviewed separately by a panel, and after their interview, they waited in a separate room until they were called back in. Once they were called back in, the panel announced that they had been approved for missionary work in the Congo.

They were flooded with all different emotions and relieved to be finally going to the Congo. They also realized they would miss their families and, more than that, that they really enjoyed their work in Kentucky, as they thought of all the children they'd loved and ministered to throughout the years. After more than ten years in Royalton, they were both

excited and nervous about leaving for the Congo.
They stayed another week in Philadelphia, ironing
out their plans with the board members. Now,
they could devote their full attention to their new
adventure in the Congo. Although their families
and some friends still tried to discourage them from
going, they refused to listen because they had a strong
calling in their hearts for the Congo. There were still
safety concerns after the war as far as the stability
outside the States. All the details had not been settled
yet, but Mae and Marie decided to start packing and
began sending boxes with things over to the Congo.
They sent their first items in October of 1945.

Several months after their items were sent, the
approval to go to the Congo came. In early 1946,
the time had finally come. The Lord was calling
Mae and Marie for missionary work indefinitely.
As they had done before, they would go wherever
God called them, and now God had a new plan and
place. But He had not called them to just anywhere
in the Congo but to remote villages where no one
dared to go. The little luxuries they had during
the depression years would be considered rich
compared to what lay in store in the remote villages
of the Congo. Mae and Marie said goodbye to their

families. They also said goodbye to Wilma and Ruth, their roommates, who had now become good friends. Mae and Marie left Royalton and took the bus to Ohio, where their church supporters would greet them and send them off. The church in Akron, Ohio, called Goss Memorial Church, would become the main support throughout Mae's missionary life. Out of that church came two couples who became good friends with Mae and Marie, Mr. and Mrs. Ray Harris, along with Fred and Ione, who were their biggest supporters, both in prayer and financially.

When Mae and Marie went to buy their airline tickets, they were not able to purchase them. The airlines said they couldn't travel overseas yet, and that only military personnel could travel back and forth out of the country. They could not believe it! They were shocked and could not understand why they could not travel. Certainly, everyone was free to travel now that the war was over. Somehow, news about Mae's dilemma got back to her co-workers at Macy's in New York and, eventually, to one of the top executives. The top executive spoke to one of Mae's colleagues, who got in contact with Mae, and asked her why she was having a problem going to the Congo. She told him the problem, and he told her he was friends with a top executive at PanAm Airlines. He asked her if they were willing to leave in a week, and if so, he could help her. She said yes, of course. To Mae's delightful surprise, he took care of everything, and the tickets were purchased.

THE MOVE

That following weekend, Mae and Marie flew out of New York. They left New York on a cold Sunday winter morning, with temperatures close to zero degrees. Mae and Marie arrived in Newfoundland, where it was also very cold. There was a two-hour layover, so they ate some warm food around a potbelly stove. They got back into the nice, warm airplane again and fell right asleep as the plane departed for Europe. Mae woke up to a bright sun over the clouds, but that soon changed to fog when they landed in Ireland. It was so foggy that the plane made several attempts to land but couldn't. Finally, after descending and ascending several times and after most of the passengers got sick and had to use the paper bags in front of their seats, the plane successfully landed. Mae and Marie were met by some barefooted priests in Ireland. Mae thought it was pretty unusual, especially seeing how cold it was. They were taken to the end of the terminal and were given some tea to drink. Soon after, they boarded again, and the plane took off. This time, they were headed for Portugal.

Mae and Marie arrived in Portugal, where they

would spend the night. They were taken by bus to a hotel. To their surprise, they were taken to a very nice hotel near the water. They stayed on the Riviera that night. That same night, they went to eat at a nice restaurant, and they had so much food to enjoy it was what seemed like a seven-course meal. They thought to themselves that this must be because of the influential executive who made the reservations for their trip. It was a once-in-a-lifetime experience they would always remember.

While on the Riviera, they met some American soldiers still stationed there in Portugal after the war. The American soldiers loved seeing Americans there. Mae and Marie enjoyed talking to the soldiers while sharing about God and the Gospel with them. After talking to the soldiers and also some of the locals in Portugal, Mae found out that Portugal remained neutral in the war. That's one reason Portugal was so beautiful and had remained untarnished by the war. Mae was also very happy to find out that Portugal was instrumental in receiving and protecting Jewish children and adults, along with other refugees fleeing Adolf Hitler's concentration camps, which were ultimately death camps. Mae and Marie were astonished by what they were hearing. The war was devastating. They thanked God that it was over and for the good that happened in the midst of it.

The following morning, they got up, ate breakfast, and drank coffee in the hotel. The hotel had big chairs that reclined. It was a little hard to eat and drink in those big chairs, Mae recalled. After breakfast, the bus took them back to the airport, where they left Portugal for Liberia. After about thirteen or fourteen hours of flying, they were finally on the continent of Africa. They were in Liberia for a couple of hours and then left for a four-hour flight and arrived in the Congo early the next morning. As they landed early that morning, Mae felt the intense heat as soon as they got off the plane. Wow! It was warm even in the early morning. It was a huge change coming from the United States and Europe, where it was very cold. Mae and Marie would land in N'dolo Airport, in Leopoldville, in early 1946. Their feet had finally touched the ground after a long-awaited six years when the Lord first called them to the middle of the bush in the Congo.

—

A LITTLE CONGO HISTORY

The Belgian Congo, located in central Africa, is the second biggest country on the continent. French has been the national language since Belgium colonized the country. Bordering nine other countries, it's one of the richest African countries due to its natural resources. It is rich in natural resources such as diamonds, gold, uranium, copper, coltan, tin, and tungsten. Over two-thirds of the country is rainforest. It has lots of rubber and palm trees, cotton, and coffee. The Belgian Congo is home to many exotic animals, including gorillas, leopards, lions, elephants, buffalos, giraffes, zebras, chimpanzees, and crocodiles. Congo's rich resources are always coveted by many foreign countries. The Kingdom of Kongo was formed as one following the alliances of several territories around 1390. The first recorded exploration from a foreign nation was in 1484 when the Portuguese explorer Diego Cao landed in the Congo River. The territory was known as the Kongo Kingdom. The Portuguese conquered and occupied the territory and turned it into a slave trade that lasted the next century.

In 1824, the slave trade was abolished due to missionaries such as Dr. David Livingston, also known as the "Abolitionist Missionary." He, along with some others, opposed and exposed the cruelness and atrocities of the slave trade.

However, King Leopold II would continue where the Portuguese left off. Between 1884 and 1907, King Leopold II enforced slave labor. It is said that he committed genocide against over ten million Congolese people. When he first arrived in the Congo, he used intimidation and submission by cutting thousands of limbs (hands and sometimes feet) off the Congolese people. King Leopold also exploited the Congolese for their rich minerals and resources. It wasn't until 1904 that a journalist from England named Edmund Morel released incriminating documents to the international community. Several missionaries, like Alice Harris from England, exposed the brutality to the world by taking photographs of the brutal reality. As a result, in 1907, the Belgian parliament conducted an investigation into the Congo. What they found out from the report made them aware of the atrocities that were occurring. They put a cease to King Leopold's reign in the Congo, which went from 1879 through 1907. The Belgian parliament took control of Congo and remained in control from 1908 to 1959.

—

Mae and Marie had long anticipated their arrival to the Congo, and it was finally a reality. It had been six years since they answered that first missionary call at the church in Royalton,

Kentucky. Now, as they got off the plane and were crossing the field towards the terminal, they suddenly heard their names being called out of a crowd, *"Miss Clark, Miss Forsberg."* Mae said to Marie, *"Who in the world knows us here? We didn't tell anyone when we were coming."* As they continued walking, they heard it again, but not until they got close to the voice did they see the person. He was the legal representative of "The Unevangelized Tribes Mission," which was the organization that they would be reporting to. There were about seven other missionaries in all that came along to greet Mae and Marie. They were in Leopoldville for a conference and heard that two missionaries were coming from the States; they had come early for the conference to greet them at the airport. They were glad to see them, and the girls were awfully glad to see the other missionaries.

The missionaries then escorted them to the mission house, where they met a couple named Mr. and Mrs. Icher. A mission house was where the missionaries stayed while working in the villages. Before they had a bite to eat, the couple asked if Mae and Marie wanted to change into cooler clothing or go in the living room for some cool water or lemonade. They decided to have some lemonade first. The couple told the ladies that, due to the weekend conference, the mission house was booked up, and there were no available occupancies. However, they did manage to find a room in the Salvation Army, which was behind the chapel, down the street from the Ichers' place. They asked if Mae and Marie minded staying there. They were fine with the arrangement made for them. Mae said, *"A room in the Salvation Army is better than the streets."* The Ichers took them there to change and freshen up before heading back for dinner. After dinner, Mae and Marie met all the other missionaries for social time at the mission house. Then, they took Mae and Marie to the Salvation Army room, where they stayed for two nights.

They got around via carts that were pushed by the local young men. The locals knew some English words, so they could communicate with the ladies somewhat when they were around. After a few days there, it was time for Mae and Marie to travel to the interior. Mr. Icher owned a truck, so he offered to drive them into the bush while Mrs. Icher stayed behind. He told them it would be a rough ride into the bush, so they knew what to expect. The drive would take a couple of days, and they were excited for their first experience in the bush life. The road was bumpy, so it took a little getting used to. Mr. Icher's eyesight had deteriorated a bit, and he wore very thick glasses, which concerned them a little, and they wondered how well he could see, especially in the evening. They seemed to be making it fine so far, and after a day's journey, they stopped at a Baptist mission. At the mission was a couple named Dr. and Mrs. Tuttle, who seemed to be very nice and pleasant and had dinner ready for them. It was there that they were introduced to their first native food. They were shown how to eat palm nuts, among other things. It was messy, but they learned how to do it pretty quickly.

They were back on the road early the next morning. They drove another day and, this time, they stayed in a sambola. A sambola is a tent house setup for travelers from out of the country, sort of like camping. Mrs. Icher had packed some sandwiches for the trip, and Mr. Icher shared them with Mae and Marie for dinner that night. Mr. Icher gave the ladies a fold-up cot to sleep on in the sambola while he slept in the truck that night.

Since it got very dark at night, he also gave them a little lantern. The next morning, they got up, gathered their things together, and drove a short way to a river. Mae thought to herself, *How is this going to work?* Little did she know, she was in for an adventure!

At the river crossing, some local men were in the water with what seemed to be just big logs tied together. There were no boats and no canoes. Mr. Icher drove the truck down a steep embankment, near where the logs were tied up with big ropes. They looked like several makeshift canoes tied together with a big flat board on top. They all got out of the truck and stood and began balancing themselves on these logs with nothing to hold on to. Mae thought to herself, *Good grief, is this how we're supposed to get around, traveling by water?* The local men rowed, standing up on both sides of the flat board, with long sticks in their hands. They were chanting in unison while rowing as the logs bobbled up and down through sometimes rough waters. It was a frightening experience!

They traveled across several rivers and saw many local villages. They saw monkeys and some other animals for the first time. That night, they arrived at a Mennonite mission village, and everyone was helpful and nice. Mr. Icher would head back from there and leave them with another missionary who was headed to the Kikwit. This was their final destination. After resting from the stressful and tiring log ride, they transferred into a van that would take them to Kikwit. They ate some type of other indigenous food, and then they left and arrived in Kikwit that evening. Since no one at the station in Kikwit was expecting them, it was a pleasant surprise for everyone at the mission once they arrived.

Mae walking in the fields with her sunhat

It felt good to know they had finally arrived after all the traveling they had gone through to get there. The locals were very friendly and happy to see them. They brought them gifts of papaya, mangos, and other fruits. When Mae took her first bite into the mango, it tasted horrible. She thought she was eating turpentine. She eventually got used to the mangos and, later, thought that maybe it was just that one first mango that must have been bad. She slowly adjusted to the local food, or maybe it was her stomach and taste buds that slowly adjusted. The days were hot, and the evenings were warm.

The river was close to them, and it attracted a lot of mosquitos. Mae and Marie enjoyed the company of missionaries like Mabel Wenger and Nettie Birdsong, who visited from another part of Kikwit. Mabel Wenger had four local children with her, and Nettie Birdsong had one. When Mae and Marie would go to their house, the children were always around, playing and laughing. Sometimes, the children tried to play tricks on them. They would sneak up slowly from behind and gently touch their feet or legs, imitating flies or mosquitos. The ladies would quickly try to slap them away, and the kids got such a kick out of that. The workers also seemed to be in good spirits. It was pleasant hearing the young workers sing as they worked. They would sing Christian songs in Kikongo, their native dialect. One familiar song they heard being sung was "At the cross, at the cross where I first saw the light." Mae could tell by the tune, even though she didn't understand the words yet.

Mae and Marie were assigned with other missionaries to assist in a village next to that one. They were there a few weeks and enjoyed helping out. They felt that there was more they wanted to do, though. There were certain guidelines the large mission had regarding how much interaction there could be with the locals. Despite the restrictions, they were grateful for the things they could do and knew there was a lot more to be done in other villages. One of the missionaries working with Mae and Marie told them of a village next to them, still in Kikwit, that needed missionaries. Mae and Marie prayed about it and felt led and believed that they would be ready for the challenge.

THE ADJUSTMENT

The new place was about two hundred and forty miles away, about a fourteen-hour drive from Leopoldville, the capital city. Mae and Marie settled at a tiny mission there after arriving by boat. There weren't too many supplies and materials to work with, but everybody was cooperative. They were told to be as careful as possible concerning mosquitoes. Malaria was relatively easy to contract, and it could be dangerous and even deadly. They were told to put a net around the bed area at night to reduce the infiltration of mosquitoes.

Although they followed the advice, no more than a month after they got there, Mae came down with malaria. Not only did Mae come down with malaria, but she came down with the worst kind. Marie had some basic medical training, but not enough to help Mae in her condition. Mae would sweat profusely until the sheets were drenched. Her body would shake so intensely that the bed would also shake. She had body aches, and she said that they hurt so much that it felt like her bones were breaking. Mae was feeling worse each day as her fever slowly got higher and higher. She had constant nausea and vomiting. After a few weeks, Mae realized that she needed immediate attention before she reached a critical and possible fatal result. The mission station told the locals to send Mae downriver to a Belgian doctor, and as the locals came to get her, they almost dropped her while putting her inside the canoe. Marie came along with Mae on the long ride to provide support and help. The trip was an all-day ride to the Baptist mission in the big village, which was a distance away from the remote villages. The ride was rough and dangerous. It was also very hot from the sun hitting the waters.

Mae had been to that mission about a month before, but this time, she was coming from the opposite direction. It was night once they arrived, and the doctor went out to the river to see Mae. He was in shock to see the critical condition she was in. The Belgian doctor was upset and felt that Mae should not have been taken by canoe since the waters were rough. He expressed that this had only made her condition worse, and she was clearly unfit to travel, especially in an unsafe canoe that could tip over at any minute. The doctor had the locals carry Mae on a stretcher that he had brought out for her. They took the stretcher to the edge of the river and took Mae back to the doctor's room in the village. He told them that when something like this happens, they should send a local runner to come to get him so he can go to her. The doctor could have gone to Mae on his riverboat and brought her back if necessary.

The doctor took Mae under his care, with a twenty-four-hour nurse for observation. The doctor mentioned to Mae that when people at a certain stage of malaria start shaking tremendously, it's referred to as "break-bone fever" because it feels as if your bones are about to break. Malaria is also known as dengue fever. The doctor asked Mae if there was anything else she needed before he left for the night, and she stated that she hadn't slept for a while now and she needed something to put her to sleep. The doctor left something with the nurse and told her to give it to her before she made her rounds. Marie stayed in the room with Mae. That evening, the nurse gave Mae a pill and told Marie that if she didn't fall asleep in the next hour or two, to give her another pill. Late that night, Mae was still awake, so Marie gave Mae another pill, but it did not work, and Mae stayed up all night.

The next morning, the doctor came in to check on how Mae was doing, and Mae told him that she did not sleep all night. The doctor said he would give Mae something that evening that would for sure have her sleeping tonight. When the doctor came in that evening, he gave Mae something to drink and said, *"This will put you to sleep; I made it myself."* Sure enough, after many sleepless nights, Mae finally had a good night's sleep. They woke Mae up in the morning so she could take her medication along with breakfast, and then she went back to sleep. They woke her up to give her medication and lunch, then she went back to sleep again, and once more for dinner, and she then went back to sleep. The same thing happened the next day. This went on for three days, and Mae slept around the clock. Mae finally woke up the fourth day and felt a little better. That night, her fever broke.

Mae started feeling her strength come back a little, but then something else happened. She began to realize she couldn't hear very well. Her ears were plugged for some reason. Mae told the doctor when he came in to check on her, and he told her that it was all that quinine she had been taking that affected her hearing. He began talking louder to

Mae because she had trouble hearing. The doctor said to Mae, *"Now, I'm going to have to start shouting at you when I talk to you,"* and Mae said, *"What's a matter with that? You don't like shouting at people?"* They both laughed. After closer examination, he realized that Mae was deaf in her right ear, but her left ear was not quite as bad. Mae's high fever finally went down, but she still had achy bones. She was now concerned about her hearing. Mae was well enough to go home later that week, and the doctor helped them return back safely to the village mission of Kikwit.

After returning to the village, she had to remain on bed rest and continued to take her quinine for a few more weeks. Mae was restless and didn't know how to stay in bed and rest for long periods of time. So, after a week, she decided that she had enough bed rest and got up. Since contracting malaria, Mae hadn't had a chance to learn anything yet. Even though they were a little intimidated, they were also excited about the challenge of trying to learn the local dialect. The language was called Kikongo. They both attempted to pursue it again, although Mae was still deaf in one ear and partially deaf in the other ear.

She became very frustrated and increasingly impatient with the hearing problem. Days turned into weeks, and then two months went by. She felt overwhelmed and discouraged, thinking her hearing would not get any better. How could she function as a missionary if she could barely hear? Her time in the Congo was done and short-lived. She was so discouraged and thought about packing up and going back to the States. Soon after, Mae received news that their missionary friends, Mable Wenger and Nettie Birdsong, wanted to take a furlough back to the States. They had not been back to the States for a few years. Mable asked Mae if she could watch the five children for her and Nettie. Marie knew about Mae being discouraged and thought this might be what Mae needed to distract her from her problems. She encouraged Mae to watch the children for a short time. Marie assured her she would be there also to help out, so Mae agreed. Around that same time, Mae and Marie were asked to work at another mission that needed help, so Mae and Marie also agreed to that.

THE FIRST ORPHANS

After Mabel and Nettie went to the States on furlough, Mae and Marie took full responsibility for the five local children while moving to another village about a half-hour drive away. Mabel had four orphans. Christine was ten, and her biological sister, Louise, was nine, Joseph was eight, and Pierre was seven. Nettie Birdsong had one girl named Mary, who was six.

Mae with the first five orphans
in her care

The kids would call Mae "Mama Clark," and they would call Marie Forsburg "Mama Fofi" because the children couldn't pronounce Forsburg. They would be known by these names for the rest of their missionary lives by all the orphan and village children. Mae would also be known not only throughout the village but throughout the region of Congo as "Mama Clark." One of the things Mae wanted to start doing with the orphan kids was devotions. She would plan it for the evenings, and this meant praying together and reading the Bible. This also meant singing worship songs to God. This was something Mae took very seriously and didn't expect anyone to miss unless there was an emergency.

This new village they were headed to was called Iwungu. They didn't have to cross a river to get to this village, but it was too far to walk there, so their missionary friends, Mr. and Mrs. Yost, took them there. They would leave for Iwungu in 1947. It was another challenging beginning. Mae wondered if she had made the right choice accepting that letter about going to a new mission. This meant she would have to start from scratch again. There was an older missionary couple there, Mr. and Mrs. Haller. They would find a temporary place for Mae and Marie until they could have their own place. The mission headquarters asked Mae if they could work on getting a school started for kids ages six through sixteen, which meant they would have to build a big house to accommodate this.

Mae thought this was a challenging task. *How could she start a school when she hadn't even learned the language yet?* To top it off, she was also partially deaf now. Could things get any more challenging? Good grief, what was she thinking? Marie said she would help out with the children while Mae worked with the locals and dealt with the school tasks. Mae decided she would take on the task of building the school. Fortunately for Mae, she would meet an eager, young, twenty-year-old man named Solomon. He had a gentle spirit and was eager to work hard. Mae eventually led him to the Lord. He worked for Mae building the school and told Mae he loved kids and wanted to be a teacher. Mae called him a godsend. Mae would come to not only trust him but bring him along to help in the different future missions.

In order to get materials and copy other things to bring back to Iwungu, she had to go back to Kikwit, which had a small school established already. She needed to get materials and copy other things to bring back to Iwungu. Mae would send a runner, who would have to ride a bicycle to pass information from one village to another. She sometimes had to wait for the head missionary at Kikwit to come to pick her up and take her to get materials when he made his rounds to the villages by car. She also worked around the clock to write down and gather curriculum information for her new school in Iwungu. Mae taught the local children reading, writing, and arithmetic. She also needed to get charts in Kikongo, which was the language that the village spoke, and the language that she would attempt to learn. The charts had words such as "ba be bi bo bu" and also included basic sentences and paragraphs. She also needed charts for math—addition, subtraction, multiplication, and numbers to one hundred. Mae had charts for this and charts for that. My goodness, so many charts! She worked really hard to get all the materials and information ready. She often took her Coleman lantern with her to use while working late into the night.

After spending several days in Kikwit gathering material from teachers there, she had a truckload of supplies for the school in Iwungu. It was a challenge trying to teach kids while trying to learn the language herself. With Solomon's assistance, Mae started the school with the orphan kids along with about ten other boys. Parents didn't permit the girls to go to school in the beginning. Mae thought if she could just get past this first difficult year, she could have a clearer vision of how to be effective with the kids and the community. She knew that once she had the language down, it would be so much easier to teach the children. Iwungu would have a school like Kikwit. In the beginning, Solomon made things possible because he knew Kikongo, and because he was very smart, he was able to learn how to teach the children. Mae would use him as her translator a lot until she was able to learn it herself after many months.

She also began to learn about village life. The local people were farmers, and they planted vegetables and beans and cassava. They also harvested some fruit trees. There was planting time and harvest time. They depended on the rainy season to grow their crops. The women worked together to grind up their grain with mortar and pestle to make flour. Certain types of leaves were pounded to make sauce, and squash seeds were wrapped in banana leaves. All these foods were eaten using one's hands and not utensils. The women would plant and prepare the food in the evening with their daughters. Both men and women were creative in making cooking pots, clothing, spears, and masks for their faces out of bark and animal skin.

A local man weaving

There were other tribes and villages where the women would do the majority of the work. This area of Iwungu was called Kifansonso.

FIRST HOME BUILT

Mae and Marie's first home was a hut built from bamboo poles. The walls and the floor were made from bamboo, and the ceiling was made from mud clay and leaves. This new hut where Mae, Marie, and the five children lived was close to the villagers. In less than a year after arriving in the Congo, for the first time, Mae and Marie were on their own, living among the villagers. They could interact more and would not have to walk as far into the village as before. The villagers appreciated how Mae and Marie showed them care and respect and made such an effort to learn more about their customs and culture. Mae and Marie were learning what to garden and what plants or trees to eat from. They raised chickens and ate rice and manioc, which is a type of flour that was brought in from Kikwit. There was a runner, who would relay messages or get materials for the villagers, but sometimes, the supplies ran out before they could restock.

Mae and Marie did not know the language well, but since the children spoke English and Kikongo, they could translate for them. The orphans had learned how to speak English from Mabel Wenger, who they had been with for several years. Mabel had been back but allowed the kids to stay with Mae and Marie to help and encourage them in their new environment. Within the village, the locals showed Mae and Marie where not to get water. There was a river a twenty-minute walking distance down the hill, where Mae and the children were warned not to go and get water from or bathe in. The river was dangerous because crocodiles would occasionally migrate there. Instead, Mae had Solomon and some other men get water from the creek, where it was safe.

The men would carry the water in buckets and bring it up to the house. This took several trips. Mae had big barrels that had to be filled to last for at least a week. Sometimes, the men carried the buckets on their heads. The water was used for drinking, cooking, washing clothes and dishes, and also bathing. The water had to be boiled under a fire in a big pot for drinking and cooking purposes. It seemed that the women learned to carry almost everything on their heads, including baskets of food, water, and other things. The younger girls also would balance large items on their heads. They would walk up a small hill while in a single file.

There were twenty to thirty villagers every day transporting items on their heads, from one place to another, all in a single file. This was one part of village life.

Marie knew a little nursing and would assist with the orphans when necessary. Marie would offer her assistance and knowledge in any way, but the villagers had their own version of medical treatment. Mae and Marie would also share the Gospel with the locals in the best way they could communicate despite the language barrier. They were careful, though, not to make it seem like they had to change their religious rituals since the villages had lots of rituals and guidelines that were regulated by the local witch doctors, who were the religious leaders in the village. These religious leaders were believed to have magical powers as they performed ceremonial rituals that had been passed on from their ancestors. They also practiced Voodoo and carried out curses if necessary.

Each village also had a chief. The chiefs didn't mind missionaries coming in to help out sometimes, especially when the village needed food. Mae and Marie were in communication with the chief of the village and understood what customs they could address and which they should shy away from. For example, all the local men and women and children did not wear what would be considered modern clothing. Most of them wore clothes made from bark from trees or a girdle of leaves around their loin area. Mae and Marie prayed that God would give them wisdom on how much and when to share with the locals. The villagers had their ritual dance in the evenings, which was a very important part of the village life. Witch doctors believed that dances performed for the purpose of communicating with the spirits would protect villagers from disease and protect crops from ruin. They also believed it gave strength to hunters and warriors in times of battle and kept communication open with their ancestors.

Their dances were very meaningful and ceremonial in nature. They were also meant for entertainment and social bonding. The women had their dances, which were precise in rhythm and timing as they worked hard at it, and the men had their warrior dances. The men were hunters and knew how to use their spears for killing animals with a poisonous substance at the end of their spear. In contrast, Mae and Marie spent a lot of time praying and reading the Bible. They rose early every morning at 5 a.m. for prayer and always had their evening devotions with their orphan children right before bedtime. The kids would wake up at 6 a.m. to do chores around the house and garden. After the morning chores, the kids would go to school. If the chores weren't done before school started, they would remain back until it was finished.

Mae would go into the village and work with the locals. She enjoyed spending time with them and learning their customs. She also aided moms when their children were ill by bringing whatever she could. She worked on building a school and getting materials sent in from Kikwit. The missions would try to get supplies for the missionaries, but it was hard to maintain. They were at the mercy of donations and shipments coming in.

FIRST SCHOOL AND CHURCH

In late 1947, the building was partially built for the purpose of serving as a school and a church. Solomon, along with Mae and the children, was temporarily outside doing things most of the time. The villagers told Mae and Marie that they were thankful and would help with any projects that were needed. Mae was anxious for the church to be built since she believed it would benefit the village greatly. There were several locals that had come to know the Lord through Mae, and she was excited to see them in church growing spiritually. Mae tried to get both boys and girls to attend school, but she found that, from the beginning, it would be difficult to get the girls to come to school. She knew that, in the villages, it was expected that girls would work in the garden and learn to cook and run the household. The locals were not convinced that girls should be going to school, but Mae would continue to advocate for the girls to participate. She believed education was just as important for them as it was for boys.

As time went by, something strange began to happen. Mae noticed that her hearing was getting better, and she could actually hear out of her right ear. She was still having problems hearing out of her left ear, but overall, it was better. Mae was still taking quinine and continued to do so for a few more months. The strength she had lost due to contracting malaria was also coming back.

Mae was glad because she needed her strength with all that was happening at home and in the community. She taught school in the daytime and then went back home in the evening to take care of the five kids. As the bamboo mud school/church was built, Mae and Marie would continue to hold a service mid-week and on Sundays. Mae would pray for revival in the village. Mae and Marie had their separate morning devotional and one together with the kids in the evenings.

They appreciated the bigger living quarters that they had, but the struggles were still difficult. One evening, they were in the living room having their devotions when they heard a noise under the bamboo ceiling. It was a crackle-like noise. They looked up, and the whole ceiling was covered with ants. These ants were known as driver's ants, and they were making their way through the walls and, eventually, the floor. Mae and Marie decided to get some matches and kerosene. They poured kerosene all around the bedposts and walls where the ants had not reached, including the floor. The devotions came to a quick stop, and everyone was sent to bed. Mae and Marie did everything they could in order to find the nest of the ants. After hours of searching and killing the ants, they finally went to bed. They were lucky that no one had been bitten, and they all slept fine and cleaned up the dead ants in the morning.

Securing food and basic necessities would continue to be a challenge, so it was time to adapt even more to village life. Mae and Marie learned to cook and make do with what they had. They learned to make bread from the flour they had by making a fire with blocks of wood, then removing the wood and setting a pan on the ground filled with the powdered flour. They would leave it in the sun for a few hours, and it would bake. They would learn the challenges of village life but also enjoy the simpleness of it. There was a town about two hours away called Idiofa, which had a little store where Mae could get food and supplies. It was run by a Belgian store owner that Mae and Marie had gotten to know. They would again show their love to the villagers and witness to them about God's love. Mae would take one or two of the orphan girls with her throughout the village to help interpret her message about God with the villagers. Mae would enjoy the beautiful evenings while she was out with the locals sharing God's Word.

In the summertime, Mae had evening camp meetings. Up until this time, she only had devotions with the children in her bamboo hut house. The witch doctor did not approve of Mae and Marie's decision to involve the people of the village in the evening services. Mae had consulted with the chiefs of the villages, and they were reluctant but granted her permission. Marie also contributed a lot to the church's growth by using the mimeograph to create pamphlets and visuals for Bible stories. Mae had wondered if she would ever get to this point, but she was making progress after a difficult, challenging start. *"Thank you, God, only by Your grace,"* she would say. The locals were learning a couple of English words, but more importantly, Mae and Marie were picking up more of the local dialect, Kikongo.

This was a good thing since she found out one day that something was not right when one of the local kids came up to her to tell her something. The boy turned his back to Mae out of embarrassment, and he was scared that he would get in trouble with the orphan children by telling on them. Mae told the boy that he needed to do the right thing and tell the truth no matter the consequences. The boy continued with his back turned to her since he didn't truly understand what Mae and Marie had said. Apparently, the orphan boys had incorrectly translated to the local kids in order to manipulate the words to their advantage. When Mae gave the local kids positive affirmation after they did something right, the orphan kids would translate to them that Mae and Marie were mad at them or that they were disappointed in them and didn't want them around. Mae thanked the local boy and told him that it was brave of him to come up and tell her what had happened. Mae shook her head at Marie and said, *"Kids will be kids."*

They realized that they needed to communicate more directly to the other local kids themselves the best they could. Mae relied a lot on the orphan children to translate because they picked up English pretty quickly and knew the native dialect very well also. Mae had a harsh talk with the orphan children about the matter. As Mae and Marie got more involved with the community and understood them more, it felt like the community was becoming a big extended family. Mae appreciated Solomon and all he was doing at the school and would hope to find and hire more helpers. Mae and Marie were also leading others to Christ.

Mae was thankful that the water supply was always taken care of, and they just needed to concentrate on the natural resources for food. Mae and Marie learned how to plant a garden and worked together with the locals planting gardens all through the village. Other than gardens, there were also papaya, mango, avocado trees, and pineapple plants. One evening, Mae was sitting in the living room, and she saw a large stick on the floor in front of the dining room table. She wondered why the kids had brought large sticks and branches into the dining room and then didn't take them back outside. She got up from her cot that she was sitting on in the living room and went to pick it up to throw it outside when the stick suddenly moved. Mae then realized it was a snake. She called for one of the kids to get a hoe so she could kill it. One of the boys, who was used to seeing snakes, came into the house and attempted to guide it back outside as the door was propped open. It was better to try to kill it outside if possible where the locals could surround it, but the snake wouldn't go out. One of the other locals heard the commotion and came to assist. They killed the snake right then and there in the middle of the living room, with a shovel.

Snakes periodically got into the house because of the high grass all around it. Mae would now be more aware of potential snakes when she was walking through the village and the house. She would not need to worry about snakes when she was being carried by kepoi, though. The villagers were capable of dealing with snakes. She would walk to visit other villagers and to her meetings at the local church and to the school since they did not have a car yet. Mae would sometimes travel to another village for revival meetings that she and one or two of her orphan girls would help out with it. While there, she would stay in a sambola, a fixture that was built with mud and bamboo. It was built like a normal home and housed officials and travelers that came through for the day and or night. Mae would take one or two of the children and set up camp for the night in a sambola similar to the one she first stayed in when she and Marie first came to the bush with Mr. Icher. She would bring necessities, cots to sleep, mosquito nets, extra clothing, a lantern, pots, pans, dishes, and bread and flour. The girls knew how to start a fire on the ground and then make bread and other foods in the pots and pans. Once in a while, Mae would go out on Friday, Saturday, and Sunday evenings to the village for revival services. The villagers would bring gifts of fruit or vegetables for Mae and the kids. Mae felt appreciated.

Mae and Marie finally were starting to pick up the language and were enjoying the village life. Mae's hearing was progressing much better and was almost back to normal. They now had a home built and a school and church building built and up and running. Right when they finally got comfortable and things were getting established in the community, they received information from another mission that there was a village in need of missionaries to help assist the villagers with their agriculture and other community needs. Mae and Marie prayed about it and felt the Lord telling them to accept their invitation. After a couple of years in Iwungu, they then moved to Mongungu in 1949.

Mongungu was located deep in the jungle and even more remote than they had ever been. One afternoon, there was a knock on the door, and as Mae opened the door, she saw a man holding a baby. He stated that he was the baby's uncle. He told her that the baby's mother had died at childbirth, and he had been able to rescue the baby but could not keep it with him. He needed to take the baby somewhere where it would be safe. The villager explained to Mae that the witch doctors had a belief that had been passed down for generations: if a mother died at childbirth and the baby was still alive, the baby had to be buried with the mother because the baby caused the mother's death. Basically, the baby has a curse on it! Mae was shocked at the ritual belief and also surprised by the request.

She looked at Marie, who had also come to the door, and they reluctantly agreed to take the baby in for its safety. However, they were not sure what they could do to keep it safe or even how they would take care of it. The first thing they did was name the baby boy David. When Mae first went to the Congo, she wasn't sure what to expect, but she did not expect much opposition from the missions.

They did not encourage missionaries to take in children but rather to assist the locals with their own children. Most missionaries were fine with that since those were not their intentions anyways. Mae, however, was open to whatever the Lord had for her, and that included taking helpless little babies and saving them from death!

I am . . .

SO GLAD TO BE ALIVE!—

and so very happy to have a place to live in,— a real HOME. My heart sings because GOD and you sent the missionaries to rescue us from being buried alive: from ignorance and superstition.

I truly THANK GOD for food and clothing, but, above all else, I thank God for
LOVE!
The love that sent Jesus to die for me; the love that caused YOU to love us enough to care for us.

Pamphlet informing of ritual

THE ORPHANAGE

Word got around that Mae and Marie's religion was different and didn't follow the belief of burying children with their mother. They prayed about the possibility of other relatives bringing babies to them because of this cultural superstition and witch doctors' teachings. They also had to deal with going against the mission's headquarters objection of not directly taking village babies in. Through the locals in this village, Mae learned additional details about rituals of babies being buried alive with their mother if the mother happened to die at childbirth. She also learned how kids and babies were cursed due to all kinds of strange superstitions and were, therefore, unwanted. Adults were also targets of curses from these witch doctors.

Mae realized that the witch doctors, along with villagers, were the victims of their own indigenous religion, and the results were, unfortunately, taking the lives of innocent babies. Mae would speak about it on Sundays and Wednesday church services with the villagers. There were many locals that were practicing these rituals, but Mae didn't have contact with them and only drew in a small percent of the villagers who would come to hear her speak. Church meetings would be part of the community events, which Mae would help organize. This would become an avenue Mae and Marie would use to reach the community while communicating and showing love and concern for the children and adults.

Outfits that Witch doctors wore

Mae checked on David constantly because he hardly cried. Being around babies a lot, she knew that something was different with this baby. As time went by, she noticed that he was developing much slower. A few months later, there was another knock on the door, and another man brought a baby for Mae to take care of. The baby had been starved because the witch doctors had said not to feed her because she needed to die and be buried with its mom because it was cursed.

Mae took the baby girl in and named her Arline. Since she did not have any cribs, Mae kept the babies in a wooden box. She would take them with her everywhere she went, always making sure to cover the boxes with nets to keep the mosquitoes from getting to them. There were so many mosquitoes in the bush, and villagers often came down with malaria.

After many months passed, a doctor came by, and he examined the babies. He told Mae that David had Down syndrome, and that was why his development was slow, even though he was growing in size. One of the first things Mae and Marie noticed was that David wasn't sitting up. Arline would develop much faster. Mae would come to develop a real love for David. He had a sweet, gentle spirit and personality. These were the first two babies Mae and Marie took in. Mae and Marie would gain the villagers' trust, so they would ask them for advice with their or their relatives' babies and children while believing that it was the right thing to do.

After some time passed, Mae heard yet another knock on the door. It was a woman who said that her sister had died, and the funeral was that evening. She went on to say that the baby would be put inside the coffin right before the mother was put in the ground. She asked if Mae could come and rescue the baby. Mae went that same hour and hid in the bushes until dusk. As the baby was being buried in the ground with the mother, Mae watched in the bushes. After a short period and the last person had left, Mae came out of the bushes and began unearthing the baby from the ground. After retrieving the baby, she quickly left and brought him home alive. Unfortunately, the baby died after a couple of days.

Mae and Marie prayed that somehow God would show the locals it was wrong to believe in the rituals of babies being cursed and having them buried alive with their mothers. This caused a lot of friction between them and the local witch doctors, and their relationship came to a climax when, one day, the witch doctors told the villagers about an eclipse that was going to happen. The witch doctors heard about it from a Catholic priest who had passed through the village. The witch doctors mentioned to the villagers that they were about to predict how the moon, earth, and sun were going to act in a certain way, and this was part of their powers. Mae and Marie already knew about the eclipse and explained to the locals the ability to know ahead of time and that it was the priest who passed the information to the witch doctors, or else they wouldn't have known.

This upset the witch doctors, and they told Mae and Marie to be careful, or they might be on the other end of their curses and voodoo. This did not intimidate them, and they continued to proclaim the truth in love. Mae and Marie knew from experience that this strong opposition from the witch doctors only represented a small minority around the villages. They were learning how to deal and adjust to these new challenges, as the Lord showed them along the way. They were there to build schools and churches, spread the Gospel, and assist the locals to a better life. Mae and Marie would continue to pray for guidance. They had pictured themselves in the heart of the Congo, and now they were right in the middle of the bush life. Mae was very determined and self-disciplined and expected the same standard from those around her.

One day, she was approached by a local who was concerned about a family member who had leprosy. Mae had heard about a case or two but never encountered a person that had it. The relative told Mae that they had been cursed by the witch doctor, so the chief of the village had ordered them out to live on the outskirts. Anyone who harbored a leaper would be put out of the village. Anyone who touched a leper or helped one would also be cursed. Mae was taken to where the leper was, and she rendered aid as best she could. She also brought along food to give him as well as any emotional and spiritual support she could provide. She knew she could not take him back to the village. In the next couple of days, she inquired among her missionary friends in the area and found out there was a leper camp run by a group of Belgian Catholics. Mae helped to transport the villagers with leprosy to the camp. After that, Mae encountered more children and adults with leprosy. She would continue to help transport them to the camp. When Mae ever came upon anyone severely sick or with a disease, she always made time to render them proper care as best she could.

After five years in the Congo, it was time for Mae and Marie to take their first furlough back to the States. They made plans to travel by ship since it was much cheaper than taking a flight back. The challenge would be bargaining with that ocean for over a month. They planned on a six-month furlough all together. They made arrangements with Nettie Birdsong to watch the children during this period of time. Nettie was glad to oblige. They boarded the ship at Matadi, which was an area off the coast of the Congo. Mae and Marie were seasick most of the trip. The trip felt like three months or longer instead of one. After arriving in the port of New York, they couldn't get off the ship soon enough. They were glad to be on solid ground again. When Mae saw the American flag hanging high, she said, *"Oh, how good it is to see old glory again."* Marie's sister picked them both up, and they stayed a week at her house in New

York. Then, they went to Cumberland, Maryland, by bus, where they both had friends, and Mae had extended family also.

After a month, they took the bus to Pennsylvania, where they both had grown up with their immediate families. After a month there, they traveled to Ohio to stay with friends who supported them from the church in Akron. After a couple of weeks there, they returned to Pennsylvania for the remainder of their furlough. Before they knew it, the time had come to get back on the ship for another long trip back to the Congo on that dreadful ocean. Mae and Marie got sick on the trip back once again. Back in the Congo, they were thankful to have spent time with family and loved ones back in the States, which gave them a new exhilaration as they continued their missionary life in the bush.

When Mae and Marie returned to the Congo, Marie went to Mongungu. Mae used Mr. Heller's car and had Impa drive her up to get the kids from Nettie's house. Impa was one of Mae's trusted helpers whom she counted on for lots of things. When Mae got to the house, she noticed that there were chimpanzees in the fields behind the house, which startled her. Mae came to the door, and Mary opened it. Mae asked where Nettie was. Mary said she had gone with the other kids but would be back soon. Mary, who was eleven years old, stated that she knew never to go outside when left alone in the house. What bothered Mae was that David and Arline were under three years old, and they were also in the house. Mae knew that Mary was very responsible, but the idea of the kids being left with only her to watch them would bother her for a while. Mae left a note saying that she had taken the kids. Mae and Nettie had agreed that Mary would stay with Mae since she was used to being with her for several years now.

One day, Mae asked the workers to fix a part of her roof, where it was leaking because of the rain. While they were fixing the roof, Mae climbed a ladder to see how things were going with the patching. Mae went to take another step, fell off the ladder, and fell flat on the ground. She was in agonizing pain, and she knew immediately that something was seriously wrong with her ankle. The workers were scared and went to get Marie. The workers thought they would be blamed for the accident and get in a lot of trouble. When Marie came to see Mae, she discovered that she was unable to walk. Marie told the workers that they would not get in trouble and that they should not worry. Marie asked Mae if she and the children could help her stand.

Mae asked not to be moved but, rather, that she just wanted to stay there for a bit. It was too painful for her to move. Marie brought a pillow and a blanket for Mae while she lay there for a bit. The workers worked frantically to get it done, thinking Mae might die there. They wanted to get out of there as soon as possible. Marie and the kids finally came and got Mae as she hobbled onto the bed. Mae stayed in bed for a few days. She would put her foot in a bucket of water for twenty minutes a few times a day, and Marie would prop her foot up and keep it elevated above her head as she lay in bed. She would repeat the same process for the next few days. After a week, Mae attempted to put some pressure on her foot by attempting to walk on it a little, but she could not.

Marie decided, along with Mae, that she needed to go see a doctor. The nearest doctor was a Belgian doctor at the former village where they came from. Mae did not really want to be taken by kepoi that far, but they insisted it was the only way to get her to the doctor's place. A kepoi is made of koala cloth, bamboo sticks, and palm leaves. Because Mangungu was in a remote area, they had no transportation system. The kepoi was the only option to get around, but it needed four men to carry it. A kepoi was also used, in many places, for carrying significant and prominent individuals. It was also used for injured people who were unable to walk. By this time, Mae's foot was black and blue, and broken blood vessels were visible on her skin. Marie felt that Mae was not improving and that she was in too much pain.

After a few weeks, Marie decided to send word to the same doctor that had seen Mae before, when she had malaria. It would be about a week later that the doctor came down to Mongungu. He looked at Mae's ankle and saw that her ankle had been broken and not sprained. The doctor told Mae she waited too long, and it would have to heal naturally. Mae realized that because it was a broken bone, the pain had not gone away, and it was taking longer to heal. Since the doctor had treated her before, he jokingly said, *"She likes to get a lot of attention."* Mae responded by saying, *"Everyone loves to get attention, don't they?"* Mae told the doctor that she had lots to do, including her Sunday and midweek service. She also was getting ready to organize a choir for the kids to sing on Christmas and Easter. The doctor told Mae she needed to stay off her ankle for a while. She was going to have to be carried by kepoi if she wanted to get around the village.

For the next two to three months, he would check back with her periodically. He also brought something for her to keep her ankle steady. She would need to keep it elevated and could not use the kepoi until he checked back with her. Mae soon realized that because she didn't get immediate care for her ankle, it never healed properly, so it would turn easily on a rock or a pothole. When this happened, she would be out of commission for a week again. This became very frustrating for her. She eventually used the kepoi to get around and then crutches, and shortly afterward, a cane. She would be fine for a few weeks or months, then re-injure the same ankle and have to start the whole process again. During Mae's recuperation in 1951, as she sat at home with her foot elevated, she listened to the battery-powered radio when she wasn't traveling around the village by kepoi.

One day, Mae was listening to the updates of the Korean War, which had started a year earlier in 1950. The conflict was between the North Korean communists, supported by China and the Soviet Union, and South Korea, supported by the United States. Mae listened to an American radio station that broadcasted news on issues and events concerning the United States. Meanwhile, Mae continued her missionary work, and she and Marie could see that God was blessing their work. As her health got better, she began to really enjoy working with the indigenous people. She felt that this was where she was truly called to, and a strong sense of belonging flooded her. Their work was fruitful, and they were seeing results. Villagers were giving their lives to God and getting baptized in the local, small stream.

As 1952 began, Mae continued to receive more babies, and with some, she didn't see the relatives since they were just left on her doorstep. A few more babies would be rescued that year. The following year, Mae had many more knocks on the door and many more babies brought to her. She had taken almost a dozen babies at this point and saved them from death. Word spread around the villages, both by word of mouth as well as through awareness at her meetings. The Lord provided day-to-day for Mae as her family continued to grow. She continued to count on help from the support in the States and sent out newsletters to potential new supporters.

On one occasion, a man brought his niece because his sister had died during childbirth. The baby was very sick, and they named her Joanne. They tried to nourish the baby back to health, but within two weeks, the baby died. Mae would remember Joanne because the baby died the day before her birthday. Mae and Marie were only taking in infants on an emergency basis, and this was a recurring theme for the next two years. Mae also noticed that it was almost always the baby's uncle that brought them to her. She had heard around town that the custom was that the dead mother's brother was responsible for raising the child. As time went on, Mae expanded the orphanage, along with her outreach in the villages and surrounding area, by involving herself more and more in her ministry in the Congo.

By 1953, Mae had received fourteen children between the ages of four months and four years of age. She also asked Mable Wanger if it was okay for Christine and Louise, who were now teenagers, to come to stay with them and help out with the infants. Mable was fine with it, and the teens were glad to help out. The names of the children were Timmy, Steven, Gary, Gaston, Ronny, Billy, Larry, Joanne, Mae-June, Lois, Paul, and Samuel. Arline and David, who had come as infants, were now toddlers. Mae had run out of room to accommodate all of them. This was the beginning of the orphanage for Mae. Her future would now be different than she had first imagined, knowing that she would be concentrating on raising orphan children of her own. Her focus had to change as she figured out how to build an orphanage to accommodate all her children.

As this new future opened up, Mae became increasingly aware of the Soviet Union and communism being a concern around the world. There were also concerns about communism being at the forefront of events and conflicts in the Congo. Mae prayed about the Gospel penetrating the difficult communist countries and so that nothing would deter the Gospel of Christ. Mae also kept up with the Korean War until it ended in a stalemate in the summer of 1953. In 1954,

Mae received a letter from Unevangelized Tribes Mission, the organization that fiscally supported her, stating that they would be folding and would no longer be in existence. This came at a bad time since Mae was going through a transition herself with the accommodation of the children. She and Marie prayed, not knowing what would happen next. Although UTB dissolved, the Christian protestant movement was growing stronger with more missionaries coming to the Congo.

The Gospel message of Christ was being proclaimed throughout, but it would take time to reach the deep and hidden villages in the jungle. Mae and Marie were determined to do their part, one soul at a time. Not more than a week later, Mae received a letter from another organization called the Congo Gospel Mission. They heard about UTB folding and offered to sponsor her and Marie. They rejoiced and thanked the Lord for providing the CGM organization that came to them and offered their support. The CGM told Mae about a mission in the area called Kintshua Mission where she could take the kids. The move was deeper into the forest, and the organization provided a car, so Mae and the kids could move from their home in

Mangungu to Kintshua. Mae and the orphanage moved to Kintchua into a hut that was too small to hold everyone.

Mae met with the chiefs of the village about building a bigger house and asked for workers to help build it. The chiefs were accommodating to Mae. They said she could build a home near the end of the village that would be on an acre of land that she could have. The chiefs also provided some workers to help them. Mae and Marie designed the new, seven-room brick house, which would be unique in comparison to the other mud huts in the village. The orphanage consisted mainly of infants, so most of the attention was given to taking care of them and not to interacting with the community as before.

After a few weeks in the seven-room brick home, Mae found herself up late one night, finishing up some tasks, and all of a sudden, she heard some noise outside the back window. She went out back to see where the noise was coming from but didn't find anything. Half an hour later, she thought she heard some loud breathing, so she went to the front windows but, again, didn't see anything. The next day, she was in the village and asked the ladies if they had a break-in or if there were people who liked to walk around late at night. The women looked at each other and said, *"Should we tell her?"* Mae looked puzzled and said, *"Tell me what?"* One of the ladies said, *"I don't think it's any of the villagers,"* but to be aware that there were leopards around the perimeter that lived just over the hills. Mae's house was next to a hill, and the hill led down to the back window of the house. She asked them how villagers usually handled this problem, and they said not to open the door when leopards came around. Mae was puzzled at their suggestion. They proceeded to suggest that she should talk to the chiefs about it and, maybe, they could suggest something more impactful. Mae was worried that the leopards would be able to smell the babies' diapers and other things from the house and want to come in.

She talked to the chiefs later that day, and they said that they hadn't seen any leopards but decided to help her anyway. A couple of the villagers, along with the chief of the village, devised a plan to trap the supposed leopard that was coming around near the back of the building. Mae went a week without hearing any noise, thinking they had killed the leopard, but the next night, she heard a scratch

on the back door window, so she quickly went to
see and shined the flashlight next to the window
and saw the leopard retreating. The next day, she
went back to the chiefs and told them what she
had encountered. They said that they laid out some
food and hoped that it would attract the leopard
away from the area.

The village chiefs

A few days later, the leopard was finally caught
and killed. Mae thanked the chief and hoped that it
would take care of the leopard issue, but she wasn't
convinced that the issue was completely resolved.

The chief had saved the leopard head and skin for himself. He told her to let him know if there were any more encounters so he could add more to his collection. Mae had a pretty good rapport with the chiefs of the villages in the area, and they worked together as much as possible.

The orphanage would continue to grow as there would be many more knocks on the door and babies to take in. Mae knew that she would be taking in more children if they needed to be rescued for whatever reason. She decided to put out newsletters in both the Congo and in the States for prayer and support. She was constantly praying for God to provide for all the children. Mae received letters back saying that they would pray for her and the orphaned children. Mae received two more babies in 1954.

Mary, who was now fourteen, had the most responsibilities taking care of the babies and kids, apart from Mae and Marie. Christine and Louise, who had stayed at the orphanage that first year to help with all the babies, went back to live with Mabel Wenger. Now, at seventeen and eighteen years old, they would go back and forth to the orphanage when Mae needed them or when they wanted to come for a brief time to help out.

A few years passed, and the babies were now young kids, four and five-year-olds running around. There was still always room for one more. David, who was three or four years older than most of the other infants, was always gentle and sweet and loved to protect his little orphan brothers and sisters. There were many kids running around that he could play big brother to.

One morning after breakfast, one of the children, named Billy, climbed up on a chair and reached for one of several bottles on the shelf. He reached into it and grabbed what looked like candy. He took it back to his bed and began eating the chewable pills and then laid down. It was soon time for lunch, and as the children were eating, Mae noticed that Billy was not at the lunch table. She asked where Billy was, and one of the children answered, *"Mama Clark, he is laying in the bed."* Mae went to check on him, and when she saw him lying down, she saw that he was foaming at the mouth. When she saw the bottle next to him, she quickly realized that he had ingested several malaria pills and quickly got Marie's attention. There was a car at the mission that they called for, and Impa took

Mae along with Billy, who appeared to be really sick, on a long drive to see the doctor. When they arrived, the doctor was with him for only a brief time, and Billy passed away. The doctor said too much time had passed since he had taken the pills and laid down when he arrived at his office. Mae broke the sad news to the family when she got home. Mae and Marie talked to the older girls about all working together to watch the younger ones better.

On another occasion, one of the children, named Janette, who was four years old, got sick. She came down with a rare disease. The doctor said there was nothing that could be done. She passed away in the summer of 1956. Later that year, Mae received another knock on the door. A man stood there, pleading for Mae to take the baby boy in. The man was the baby's uncle. Mae agreed to take him, and the uncle came back the next day with the twin girl. The man wasn't sure if Mae would take two babies in at one time, so he thought that if Mae took the one baby, then realized the baby had a twin, she would not turn the second baby away after receiving the first one. The twins were named Jack and Jacqueline.

One day, Mae received a letter from the new organization that was supporting them called Congo Gospel Mission, and they told her that they realized what she was trying to do and that they would back up her project to build a bigger orphanage in a place called Kalanganda, about a couple of hours drive away. The possibility of having a place that sat on several acres was now possible. The Congo Gospel Mission backed Mae and supported what she was doing for the children. She looked forward to the new home, where she and the children could stay more than just a couple of years before outgrowing it. Mae was happy!

By the end of 1956, Mae began preparing for the big move to Kalanganda. She had a short time to move from Kintchua to Kalanganda, and it seemed impossible to build a home that would fit all the kids in such a short period of time. Mae left with some of the workers to Kalanganda for a week while Marie stayed back with the kids. They cleared brush and dirt to make way for a big house to be built. Then, she went back to get ready for the transition while the workers finished up with the smaller temporary house. The main, larger home would be built by the summer of 1957. When it was done, it took a few days to get all fifteen children transported from Mongungu to Kalanganda. Mae, with the help of the Congo Gospel Mission, began building the house in Kalanganda. Marie would not follow Mae to Kalanganda this time! She felt called to go on a different mission. Although they would see each other now and then and remain friends, it was difficult for them to part after working together for almost three decades.

Mae was able to meet the chief at Kalanganda. They had a pleasant conversation, and each showed respect for the other. The chief was so amazed by Mae and what she was doing that he granted her a total of almost four acres that would be hers to do as she pleased. She and the children lived in a small bamboo house until the bigger home was built on the large facility grounds. Mae knew she would need to find some good village workers to help because she could not do it all on her own. She was not aware at the time, but it would be important to have good-spirited workers. Mae had workers already, but she hired two more workers to help with the orphanage. The two young men were in their mid-twenties, and they would become long-term workers for the orphanage.

Mae sitting down for dinner in
the dining room with some of the
younger children

Pierre was the cook, and he grew the garden
along with tending to the animals (chickens, goats,
etc.), and Jack was the driver and maintained the
facility grounds. Solomon, who had been with Mae
for some time now, was the lead teacher at the
school in Kalanganda. Within the next couple of
years, Mae took in several more children. By 1958,
Mae had twenty-nine children in her care. Mae
continued to count on support from friends and

churches from the States. She sent out newsletters and cards each year. After a couple of months, she received a gift from the supporters from the States, which was enough to purchase a large vehicle, the size of a small school bus. It had no seats, but you could just put kids in side by side and fit twice as many. Mae called the vehicle Goliath.

That same year, Mae hired two more workers for the orphanage, Charles and Epiongo. They were also loyal, hard workers. They would help with driving, teaching, and working on the school building. In 1958, Mae prepared for her oldest orphan, Mary, to be married that year. Mae joked that Mary's future husband could stay there, and they could both help raise the children, so the marriage was perfect timing. Mae would miss Mary, not only because she was so helpful and responsible but also because she was a good Christian and the most respectful kind of daughter that she could have ever asked for.

Things were going well in the Congo, and Mae continued to help out in the community. The orphanage did not hinder Mae's community work as she had previously thought it would; she just had to make some adjustments to maximize her time.

Mae hired the same workers that built her house to work on building the school. The school building was built in six months. By now, Mae had a good grasp of the language, which made things easier.

The school had around seventy-five kids from the age of four to sixteen years old. Both boys and girls went to school. Mae didn't need to be a teacher, but she really enjoyed it, so she still taught in Kikongo on Sundays and Wednesdays, in the school/church building that was on the grounds of the four acres she owned. She also decided to teach an adult class for those young men and women that wanted to go into the ministry. Impa and his girlfriend attended along with a young man named Andre, who was planning to attend the seminary in the near future. During Belgium's rule, they had colonial restrictions on education. Basically, no Congolese citizen could become a doctor, lawyer, or engineer. Mae encouraged her children and other Congolese men to pursue an education in what they were allowed to pursue. Mae, especially, encouraged them to become pastors or teachers.

The river in Kalanganda was not as dangerous to get water from as it had been in the past when the river was shared with wildlife. Mae would use this river to baptize her children along with the villagers and their children. After school, the children would come home and get their chores done before dinner. After dinner, they had their schoolwork to finish.

Before bedtime, the family would gather together for their nightly devotions. Mae would use flannel graphs and props when telling stories so kids and grownups would have a visual to better understand what the stories were about. She had adult and child-sized flannel graphs of New and Old Testament characters. For instance, she had Jesus and the disciples, David and Goliath, and so on. The children would also remain active in the community by putting on plays. Mae loved telling Bible stories at home and in the community.

Kalanganda was a beautiful home with many palm trees along with open and endless green land as far as the eye could see. There was lots of room for the twenty-nine kids to enjoy and have fun! The house was on higher ground, where you could see for miles around, with jungle all around in one of the largest green rainforests in the world.

"Mama Clark" with her girls
in the backyard with a beautiful
backdrop of the forest

Mae would once again enjoy her interaction
with the locals and village life. The village farmers
grew many crops, including beans, vegetables, and
tomatoes. Mae also grew vegetables in her garden.
She sent out for rice and manioc flour, and she
stored some for the dry season. Mae discovered
that one of the favorite foods she enjoyed with the
orphan kids was called fufu. It was a white, dough-
like shaped ball made from cassava flour. They ate

it with sauce and cooked cassava leaves. The sauce was called saka saka, and you ate with your hands. You could make a big enough pot to have leftovers for days. The villagers would eat three times a day, when possible, and noontime was the biggest meal of the day.

It was rarely cold in the Congo; it was mostly really hot and sometimes warm. The sunrise was a sight to see as it came up over the hills and palm trees. The sunset, in the evening, hit the backyard with a shimmer of light, and one could see the jungle for miles. There was a sense of adventure and hope and renewed dreams for the future of the Congo. Mae's compound had the potential to expand, if need be, for more orphaned children. Mae envisioned large schools for the kids and training rooms for potential teachers. Mae was also excited because it seemed like the locals were so eager to hear about the Gospel. Amongst the busy life and accomplishments that were happening, Mae realized how short life could be when she received a letter in June of 1959, notifying her that her mother had passed away. It was hard for Mae not to be able to be there with her family to mourn the deep loss. The children would be Mae's comfort.

One day, Mae had a meeting with the village chiefs in Kalanganda. She shared with them her goals and needs for Kalanganda. They thought that she might be taking on too big of a project but reluctantly agreed to most of her requests. Mae and the orphanage also celebrated the first friend and worker getting married, Impa. Both he and his wife would continue to work at the orphanage while pursuing ministry and hopefully going to seminary and becoming church pastors one day. There were also two young married couples that she was training for leadership in ministry, and she hoped to continue to help train many more.

CONGO'S INDEPENDENCE

From 1957 to 1959, there had been civil unrest throughout the country. There had also been rumors of major changes and cries for independence from Belgium during this time. There were riots in the Congo resulting from the Belgian government still being in power. The Congolese people felt oppressed and stifled by the lack of progress. The political leaders and citizens demanded the withdrawal of the Belgian government and leaders. The Belgian government was reluctant, believing that it would lead to an unstable and unprepared country. Belgium's federal parliament government had ruled since 1908, but the Congolese were ready for their independence.

The Congo fought for and gained its independence on June 30th, 1960. The country was now called the Republic of the Congo. Mae was happy for the Congo to have its independence and for the freedom of the Congolese people to rule themselves after years of being subjected to cruelty and submission. Unfortunately, violence stemming from not only the two hundred different ethnic groups in the Congo but also from political leaders fighting for power began within the same week of Congo's independence. One political leader named Moise Tshombe decided to take his region, where he had political support, and broke away from the Congolese government to establish his own government, therefore, naming himself President of Katanga. This was in the south part of the Congo, where the capital city was Elisabethville. Leopoldville was in the west part of the Congo, where the central government, headed by Kasavubu and Mobutu, and the Congolese military resided.

Also, during this time, Congolese troops decided to revolt against their White Belgian officers. With the intention of restoring order and protecting European lives, Belgium troops mobilized their forces in the Congo while flying in more troops into the country. The Belgian military action was interpreted by the newly independent Congo as an attempt to re-impose Belgian authority and continue domination. This infuriated the new Prime Minister, Patrice Lumumba, who had most of his loyalists and support in Stanleyville, which was in the northern part of Congo. Lumumba needed help to fight the opposition and asked different foreign powers for military assistance. From his request came misinterpretations and mistrust, which resulted in the leading parties fighting for power, and other parties, who were excluded from the race, fighting for power, also. The reaction put all foreign personnel on notice, which caused the UN to respond immediately. The UN began to send peacekeepers to help evacuate all foreigners. Mae had been made aware of all the latest occurrences happening in the Congo and was told she also had to evacuate. The locals, who were friends with Mae, promised that they would look after the orphans. Mae told the kids to take care of each other and that she would be back soon. She entrusted some of the local adults to look after the children while she was gone.

There were rumors that some missionaries and other foreigners had been killed while fleeing by train from the Congo to the border. There was word of bloodstains found in the boxcars of the trains. The UN helicopters came and evacuated Mae back to Leopoldville. It was always difficult for Mae to leave the children. In mid-1960, Mae left the Congo and went back to the States for safety reasons. While Mae was in the States, she took time to visit family and friends in

Pennsylvania, along with friends and other relatives in Maryland. As Mae was keeping a close ear on what was happening in the Congo, she heard that the UN secretary-general employed UN military forces all throughout the Congo and demanded all Belgian forces to withdraw all of their troops back to Belgium. It was the beginning of UN troops in the Congo.

Within the next four years, there would be up to almost twenty thousand UN troops from many different countries to help keep the peace in the Congo. Not only were there leaders from different parties fighting for power, but the Cold War between the United States and the Soviet Union would also play out in the political affairs of the Congo. While Mae was still in the States, near the end of her stay, she was able to listen to the debate between the two presidential candidates, Kennedy and Nixon. Mae heard them mention the Congo and its internal conflicts. She prayed that America would take concern of the Congo for the right motive and attempt to intervene in order to help resolve the conflict at hand and to help stabilize the situation to keep the peace. Mae was hoping that the Congo would be able to settle the conflict and make the transition to independence on its own. The political leaders were making it more difficult by fighting for power and causing the country to be divided, resulting in a civil war.

In November, after several months, and after being notified that she could resume her missionary work, not knowing that the conflict had not been totally resolved, she flew back to the Congo. Mae was the first White missionary to enter back into the province of Bandundu, where she was welcomed back as if she was royalty. When Mae returned to the compound, she was glad to see that the children were alive. Unfortunately, they had not been taken care of as she hoped they would be. The locals asked Mae if she wanted them to stay and continue the help on the compound. Mae turned down their offer, especially since the children said that they had basically taken care of themselves for the most part. The children were noticeably thinner and not in great shape. Now that Mae was back, she hoped that things would settle down. The transition to independence was not going as smoothly as hoped, but she was very thankful for Congo's independence. Hopefully, now there would be fewer limitations on the Congolese people to pursue personal endeavors and accomplishments. The Congo had a good infrastructure left for them by the Belgians, as far as hospitals, schools, airports, railroads, and industries were concerned. Mae hoped that whoever was elected president would really have the best interest of the Congo.

In 1961, Mae heard on the radio that President Kennedy supported the United Nations being in the Congo. Hopefully, this would help keep the peace, and all other countries would stay out of the Congo military's way so the UN could do their job successfully. Mae hoped that it was true about the UN being able to keep the peace. She also knew that the Congolese citizens were not happy with foreign intervention and how they handled and were continuing to handle the conflicts in the Congo. Many Congolese citizens seemed to be divided in the matter. Mae was the only White missionary in the region to return until other missionaries returned to the Bandundu Province later in 1961.

Certain events at Kalanganda would help take the attention of what was going on around them. Solomon's wedding was a good excuse to celebrate some normalcy again. Now a full-time administrator, Solomon remained a good friend to Mae and continued working with the orphanage. Things seemed to calm down, but Mae felt a constant uneasiness in the political atmosphere. In late 1962, Mae was listening to the radio news and became concerned with the crisis between America and the Soviet Union and the potential nuclear showdown. Mae and the older children would pray for the situation to get better. At the same time, trouble was starting up again in the Bandundu region in late 1962.

One afternoon in early 1963, as she was doing the afternoon chores, she began to feel sick. All of a sudden, she was having trouble breathing, and she felt her heart pounding rapidly. She sat down on the couch to rest and to try to catch her breath. She felt worse, so she then laid down on the couch. The next thing she saw was a light in the distance, but around her, it was completely dark. Then, the light started getting closer to her until there was color all around her! She, then, saw herself lying down on the couch, and she began to wonder if it was her time to go. She looked into the yard, where all the kids were playing, and said to herself, *"What about all of these children? Who will take care of them?"* At that same time, Impa walked by and saw that something was wrong. He noticed that her face was pale white. That sent Impa into a panic. He repeatedly said, in Kikongo, *"Mama Clark, Mama Clark, are you okay? Please wake up!"* He shook her shoulder a couple of times, and as he attempted to shake her a third time, Mae suddenly opened her eyes. Impa, then, told Mae that she was pale white and needed to go for medical care. Mae said that she felt fine now and just needed to rest on the couch for a bit. She told Impa after he continued to insist on getting medical help that he need not worry; she just needed to rest. Mae believed that she had an out-of-body experience and that the Lord could have taken her, but because of the children, the Lord allowed her to remain and carry on the rest of the work that He had called her to do.

Another incident happened a few months later with one of the orphan children. The kids often played outside, and the boys would climb trees and play soccer in the large yard in the compound. One particular day, the boys were climbing and playing games in the trees when all of a sudden, Ruben, who was seven years of age, fell out of the tree and landed on a rusty tin can. Mae's concern was whether he had a broken limb or not. It was later discovered that he had an infection in his leg. Surprisingly, by the time it was realized by the doctor, the infection had spread, and before anything could be done, it was too late, and Ruben died from the infection. Mae and the children were very saddened by the loss. She felt bad that they had not caught the infection earlier. She and the children took time to mourn his death, and it took some time before they were able to move on from the tragic loss. Even with the pain of losing Ruben, she also had to think about the current circumstances and events in the community and region.

In mid-1963, Mae heard rumors about communist-backed rebels in the villages nearby, who were planning to start a revolution to overthrow the government. She heard that the rebels wanted to eradicate American citizens. Mae was anxious, not knowing if these rumors would play themselves out in the next six months or not. Later that year, in late 1963, Mae heard about the assassination of John F. Kennedy. She was saddened and concerned about the tragic event that took place in Dallas that November. She had little time to ponder what was taking place in the States, though, with all that happening around her region.

In December of 1963, a local man came to the orphanage and told Mae that there was trouble in the region and that all the White people would have to leave the region.

THE REBELLION

In January of 1964, rebel soldiers had moved into the region where the orphanage in Kalanganda resided. They were stationed all around the compound. They threatened Mae if she ever compromised the rebel soldiers in any way. The soldiers were there for a few weeks before Mae was rescued by the UN. She had to leave the children behind by no choice of her own. The UN's first attempt to rescue Mae was unsuccessful. The UN was not certain why Mae had not been at the designated rescue point the time before, but they decided to make another attempt to rescue her. They dropped notes from an aircraft notifying her of another attempted rescue for the next morning. There were four helicopters, escorted by two planes this time. As Mae saw the helicopters land in front of the compound, she told the children that she would be back for them. As Mae came out of the house, two soldiers with guns drawn came out to meet her and ushered her into the other helicopter.

The children were left in the house with some of the people in the nearby village that Mae had left in charge. As Mae was being flown to her destination, she asked why the children could not come with her in the other helicopters. There was plenty of room for all of them. Mae was told by the UN official that his orders were to only take her and that she would have to take up the issue of evacuating the children later with the UN or the prime minister. Mae was evacuated to Kikwit, not the nation's capital of Leopoldville, where she was first told that she would go and speak with the prime minister. After landing in Kikwit, the UN official told Mae that plans for rescuing the orphans were still in effect to take place within the next couple of days.

Mae had a list of names of all her children for the rescuers to have when they evacuated the children. Mae anxiously waited for word that the UN would rescue her children. The next day, the UN official went to see Mae and told her that the evacuation had been planned to take place the next morning. He also reluctantly told her that some of the UN helicopters had been shot down due to local battles in the region against the communist-backed rebels led by their leader, Mulele. Because of this latest development, he told her that there weren't enough helicopters for the rescue of the children. There was no way for the children to be evacuated from the compound! They were called Mulele rebels. Therefore, there would not be enough helicopters for the rescue of the children. Mae's children could not be accommodated.

The UN official also told her that they would still do as much as possible to assist with the children's rescue if time allowed them to figure out the logistics. Mae's heart sank, and it was the worst feeling she had experienced in her life. She regretted so much leaving the children. She felt that if she was still with them and had demanded that their rescue be conditional with hers, maybe they would have agreed. They told Mae that she was safer going to the capital, Leopoldville, until things calmed down. Mae knew there were other immediate concerns throughout the Congo in the different regions that the prime minister and the UN would be tied up with.

One major concern, Mae found out about later that year, was a rise in communist-backed rebels holding Europeans and Americans hostage. American C-130 aircrafts were sent out carrying Belgian troops to help assist with the hostage crisis occurring in Stanleyville. Moise Tshombe, who was the current prime minister and previous president of the Katanga province, took the responsibility of organizing a plan to both rescue and evacuate the hostages. The Belgian troops, along with Congolese troops, executed the plan and rescued hostages while killing a few communist-backed Simba rebels, who now controlled most of the region. Many of them were able to retreat back into the forests.

Unfortunately, there were many hostage casualties, and among them were missionaries along with other American and Belgian citizens. There were also between one to two thousand refugees, which included Congolese citizens. The refugees that were foreigners were flown from Leopoldville to Belgium and then to the United States. Those that had been killed were also flown back to their countries. The US Marine Guard of Honor draped American flags over the coffins of two American doctors that were flown back to the States. In the month of November, the rescue project took four days to complete. Right after that, in early December, Prime Minister Tshombe flew to Paris for a meeting with French President

Charles de Gaulle, then went on to the United States to meet with the United Nations. The hope was to have foreign support in order to end these insurrections around the country.

After the prime minister returned to the Congo, Mae was finally able to meet with him. She was able to secure an audience with the prime minister and accepted an invitation to his home. She asked him if he would consider helping her. The prime minister explained to Mae some of the events and challenges he'd been encountering around the country. Mae understood that the rebellion was at a bigger scale than she imagined. The rebels, who were being backed by Communist China, had troops as far north as Paulis, which was above Stanleyville and south of the Bundundu region, where the orphanage resided.

It seemed like the rebellion had engulfed at least half of the Congo's territory, but he would try to do all he could, within his power, to help Mae evacuate her children from Kalanganda. There was a plan to send her friend, Pastor Dhanis Nkwasamba, who was very familiar with Mae and the kids, along with UN personnel, to carry out the rescue attempt. A few weeks later, the plan was supposed to be executed but could not because the rebels were still very much in control of that area, and Prime Minister Tshombe did not have the military resources needed to defeat the rebels in that region. The rescue mission for the orphans, therefore, would once again be postponed.

Meanwhile, Mae was told not to make any attempts to go to the region where her orphanage resided, or she would be endangering her life. She was in the dark about what was happening in the compound, and the only thoughts consuming her mind were about the status of her children. Mae remained steadfast in prayer.

December of 1964 was the worst Christmas she ever experienced, filled with emptiness and grief. She decided to go live at Nettie Birdsong's house, her long-time missionary friend. Nettie had traveled to the States and became ill but got better and was living back in the Congo. There were some other missionary friends that Mae would turn to for emotional support and would also remain in contact with during her long wait in Leopoldville. Mr. and Mrs. Yost, Viola Anderson, Aunt Ruby, Miss Brae-man (from Switzerland), Ray and Margaret Bobecker, Vanete Hancock,

Paul and Teresa Chaponaire, Mr. and Mrs. Grings, Mr. and Mrs. Haller, and Mae's best friend, Marie, were among some of them.

Mae heard the news about a certain rebel leader that had been around the compound and had been captured and had supposedly been killed by the national soldiers. This rebel leader, who resided in the south, was one of the three main rebel leaders. The other two were in the central and northern parts of the zones where the fighting was taking place. Mae was on her knees in constant prayer all throughout the rebellion. She was very concerned for her children. She knew that the boys, once in the hands of rebel soldiers, could be brainwashed and forced to become rebel soldiers, becoming killers at such a young, innocent age.

She thought of David (her orphan boy who had Down syndrome) and how scared and helpless he would feel. He had such a good heart, and he loved and protected the other orphan children. Who would be there to protect him now? Mae was also concerned for the girls, knowing they could easily be raped and murdered by rebels or angry villagers.

Mama Clark with David and two orphan girls in the backyard

Mae felt so alone and helpless. She leaned on the scriptures she read and memorized throughout the Bible. It's what kept her going and gave her hope. Mae would read the Word in the morning and evenings, as she often had when going through difficult times of growth and in moments of victory. Mae had many key verses from the Bible that she loved and would memorize them to sustain her during perilous times. One of Mae's favorite verses was Psalm 121:1–3, 5–8, which says:

"I lift up my eyes to the hills, where does my help come from? My help comes from the Lord, the maker of heaven and earth. He will not let your foot slip; he who watches over you will not slumber."

"The Lord watches over you. The Lord is your shade at your right hand. The sun will not harm you by day nor the moon by night. The Lord will keep you from all harm. He will watch over your life. The Lord will watch over your coming and going, both now and forevermore."

Some of her other favorites were: Joshua 1:9, 22:5; Psalms 3:4, 9:10, 46:1, 91:1–2; Proverbs 22:6; Isaiah 12:2–4; Jeremiah 29:12–13; Matthew 10:16, 11:28, 18:19–20; Mark 9:41, 10:45, 11:23–24; Luke 15:7, 10; John 1:12, 3:16, 5:24, 15:7–8; Acts 1:8; Ephesians 1:7, 11, 3:20; Hebrews 6:10, 11:6; 1 Peter 2:9, 3:18; 1 John 2:15, 5:12–15; Revelation 3:20. Mae would keep all these verses and meditate on them, not only through this difficult time but throughout her life.

Days turned into weeks, and weeks turned into months. A year had passed since she had been evacuated, and Mae finally heard some news about her compound. It was reported that the compound had become a war zone. Her worst nightmares had come to life when she was told that some bodies of small children were found around the compound where her house resided. Mae hoped that none of the bodies found would be any of her children. She also heard that young women had been raped. One girl that Mae knew had been raped in the village near the orphanage. The compound had totally been destroyed and turned into a battleground. That's one reason why the UN did not want Mae to see the devastation left in the aftermath.

The war had driven the refugees into the jungles and forests. Those who could run hid and found food and shelter in any way they could. They tried desperately to avoid being injured or killed by soldiers, rebels, wild animals, or being captured and raped. Mae wondered whether any of her children could have survived. Despite her worries, Mae was not permitted to leave the city of Leopoldville to go to Bandundu province. The children were in a war zone at the time, and it was unsafe. Kalanganda was the area where the rebels resided for over a year and where the military soldiers were at war there with them. Mae continued to plead for intervention, but she was told it was just too dangerous and very difficult to pursue at the time.

Mae was prompted by friends and officials to abandon the idea of a rescue of the children. Mae was fifty-six years old at this time, and she had done twenty years of missionary work in the Congo. Mae prayed for God to show her and tell her what to do. Some people told Mae that even when the rebellion was over, it would be very difficult to pick up from where things had been since there had been continual fighting in the Congo. There had also been over one hundred thousand lives taken. That number included soldiers and civilians, including the Congo's first prime minister and the UN secretary-general. In spite of the circumstances, Mae did not feel at peace about leaving the Congo. She still felt a desire to continue with missionary work, and she was not going to give up on the children.

She began to work on finding a place to start over. This would keep her occupied for the next year or so while waiting to hear any news about her children. During this time, she continued to reside at Nettie's home. One day, Mae was called to the door, and there stood a man with a baby in his hands; and he asked Mae if she was still taking babies in. The baby's mother, his sister, has died during childbirth. This was all too familiar for her! Mae refused and said that she had no place of her own and was not equipped with supplies to take care of the baby. She wondered how the gentleman had found her since she was at a new place where no one knew her. The man continued to plead for Mae to take the baby in. There were some other missionary girls visiting that happened to be at the house at the time, and they told Mae that if she took the baby, they would help out in any way that they could. The girls insisted that she take the baby in, and she reluctantly did so. The missionary girls wanted to name the baby Teddy.

He looked like a little, shriveled, wrinkled old man, but they insisted he looked like a little teddy bear. The youngest missionary girl gave Mae her doll carriage to put Teddy in. Mae immediately took him to the doctor in town, and he told her that there wasn't much he could do to save him. Regardless of what the doctor said, she began gathering the necessary items to accommodate him, even though she knew that he didn't have much of a chance of surviving. For the next couple of weeks, Mae took extra care of him, feeding him day and night.

Miraculously, over the next couple of months, he made a full recovery. So much so that when Mae took him to see the doctor again, he didn't recognize the now chubby baby. Mae wasn't expecting to have relatives of babies in danger searching for her in the city, but soon she would find out that the pattern would continue.

Mae with Teddy, the first baby she took in while living in the city in 1965 during the rebellion

Eventually, there was another knock on the door. It was another gentleman with a baby girl whose mother had died. He asked if she could please take her in because there was no one else to take care of her. Mae took the baby in, figuring she already had one baby, so she already had what she needed, and it would be easier to take care of her. This baby girl was named Kay. Mae had a special bond with the babies, and they reminded her even more of the children that were gone. She felt the void and emptiness along with the overwhelming pain of her other children, who were still missing.

These new babies would comfort Mae and help with the pain and anxiety she felt. A couple of weeks after receiving the babies, some pastors came to Mae, telling her that they had heard that she had received some more babies and wished to continue her orphanage in the city. They also told her that a vacant store in the downtown area had become available and asked her if she was interested in staying there until she found a permanent place.

At first, Mae was not sure about the idea of staying in a temporary store in the city since it was the total opposite of the house she came from in the forest, which had several acres of land. Where would she put all the children once they were found and returned to her? Mae prayed about the situation and felt led to live in the temporary store while trusting that the Lord would take care of the situation when the time came. In the summer of 1965, Mae received a letter from the US informing her that her older sister Clara had passed away. She was very saddened by her sister's passing and knew she could not leave to go back for the funeral. She hardly even had time to grieve with so much going on.

Soon after, Mae received another knock on the door. This time, it was military personnel that told her that she needed to go to the government office. She knew that it had something to do with the missing children, so she went right away. While Mae was waiting to see the prime minister, she met a lady passing by that worked in the government building whose name was Marguerite. Marguerite sat down and briefly spoke with her. She was sympathetic to Mae's situation and listened to her story. Marguerite proceeded to tell Mae that there were a lot of issues and events that had occurred in the country, especially in the last five years, since the Congo's independence. There were political parties and politicians fighting for power and influence, and outside influence from different countries, also trying to impose their influence militarily and economically.

Marguerite said that this was not unfamiliar territory for the Congo due to its past history. She said that she remembered the events that took place during World War II. She recalled when Hitler and the Nazis conquered Belgium. During Nazi occupation in Belgium in 1940, they tried to impose control over Belgium's other territories, including the Congo, since it was highly sought after because of its rich and vast natural resources. While the Congo remained neutral at the beginning of the war, the Nazis were able to confiscate large amounts of diamonds to contribute to their war effort.

The United States also made sure they were not excluded and were able to acquire large amounts of Uranium for building bombs in their war effort. The British government had deep concerns and got involved. The British government was concerned that the Belgian Congo might eventually side with Germany. The British government threatened to invade the Congo unless they pledged all their resources to the Allies and their war effort. The Belgian Congo reluctantly gave in and sided with the Allies and assisted with military aid and resources.

Marguerite stated that, unfortunately, the Congo would always be an interest to foreign establishments because of Congo's abundance of rich natural resources. Marguerite wished Mae the best and told her to let her know if she could be of help in any way. When Mae went to talk to the prime minister, he stated that the military was gaining back control in that region, but it would still take more time until it was under complete government control. He wanted to personally give her an update and assure her that he was doing his best to secure the rescue of her children and had not forgotten her request. The prime minister also told Mae that he had heard about her needing a bigger place when she got the kids back or started anew. He told her that there was a piece of land that he would make available for her when she was able to afford to buy it.

Within a few months, Mae was notified that the rescue attempt of the children could move forward. The UN, with the assistance of Pastor Dhanis, would go and help with the efforts to rescue the children. Mae gave them a list of the children's names so they could look for each of them individually.

Pastor Dhanis next to a soldier as they were escorted by UN personnel during the rebellion while attempting to rescue Mae's orphan children

Mae was concerned because, since so much time had passed, she didn't know what the children looked like anymore. By the time Mae was notified that the UN, Red Cross, and Pastor Dhanis were approved to commence the rescue, the prime minister was out of office, but the mission was still approved to move forward. The next morning, the UN truck left for the Bandundu region, and, as had been planned, once the military gained control, with the help of the UN and the Red Cross, the rescue mission was on!

The UN truck arrived in the Bandundu region in the late morning and began searching for the children. The plan was to search each village in case they had been misplaced and call out each name. After the first day of going through villages and calling out names and asking around, they came up empty. Mae continued to maintain hope, not knowing what conditions the orphans would be in when found. Mae hoped for the best but prepared herself for the worst. She knew she would not give up looking for the children until she could account for each one of them. For the next few weeks, the UN would make several trips to the Bandundu region looking for the orphan children. They also looked into Red Cross hospitals, but nothing turned up.

It took several more trips and searches through the villages, with the help of the Red Cross, until the first orphan finally appeared. Ronny answered and came running towards the truck. After that day, one by one, there would be other orphans who would answer to their names. Unfortunately, it happened few and far between. Over the next couple of years, a few of the children, who had managed to stay alive, showed up at Mae's front door with the help of both the UN and Red Cross. Each reunion was an emotional and happy occasion that gave Mae hope that she could find all of them.

The long journey of her children returning home began in December of 1965. One by one, each time she met them at the door, she could not believe it; she thought she was having a dream. They were hardly recognizable, having gone through a combination of hunger, persecution, and sickness. They were filthy and thin. In the next few months, more rescue trips would take place, and more children would be found. By the end of 1967, thirteen of her children were back with her. There were sixteen children still unaccounted for, and Mae had to come to terms with accepting that the missing children were possibly killed in the rebellion.

The children who were found within two to three years from Mae's evacuation from Kalanganda were: Tim, Sam, Gaston, Ronny, Gary,

Joy, Dorothy, Bobby, Jacqueline, Jack, Gideon, Mae-June, Dale, and Jimmy. David, the boy with Down syndrome, would be amongst those that did not return to Mae and the orphanage. She would continue to mourn his absence along with the other fifteen children that had been missing for over two years.

All the children were very ill when they came back from the rebellion. Mae had to put Mae-June in the hospital right away, while the UN went back to search for the remaining sixteen children in the Bandundu province. They made a couple more trips but did not find any more children. It was officially recorded that sixteen children had been lost. Mae would still hope in her heart that the missing sixteen would one day miraculously appear on her doorstep. She knew with God, anything is possible. Mae was still unsure whether her surviving children would remain alive after the condition they were brought in. When they arrived at their new temporary vacant store, she was able to tend to each of them, especially those who were still in serious condition. Some were more physically critical than others, while some were emotionally and psychologically traumatized.

Mae-June would not regain her physical health and, therefore, passed away.

For the next few years, Mae would hope to see one of her missing children come walking through the door. She couldn't bring herself to have a funeral for those that were missing, believing that they could walk up to the door one day. She always wondered how each of the sixteen children had died. Was it wild animals like leopards, cheetahs, boars, snakes, lions? or were they caught in the crossfire between the military and the rebels? or was it because they were raped or contracted a disease or starvation?

It was all too much and too hard to think about, but with the help and strength of the Lord, Mae would get through the hardest time of her life. She could see the eyes of the children and see the look of war and terror on their faces. Their bodies remained thin. Their minds were traumatized, and, as a result, it would be challenging trying to ever get back to a normal environment. They lost a lot of ground, as far as schooling was concerned, being out in the forest for a couple of years. Mae thanked the UN, government, military, and the Red Cross for all of their efforts concerning the rescue of the children. She and the children had a very special and emotional church prayer and worship ceremony for those that were still missing.

Mae was anxious to get settled in the new place, which was a temporary vacant store. She began to see the children coming back to health. One by one, they began to heal both physically and emotionally. However, it was still a struggle to adjust to everyday living. They all had been through so much during those two years. The children were also getting caught up with their schooling now that they were in the city. However, school was the last of Mae's worries since their emotional and psychological needs were the priority. She would now hope for their complete recovery. For these children, the rebellion was technically over, but they still faced obstacles caused by it. There were still pockets of fighting that would continue throughout 1967 in the Congo. There was still a slight chance that the other children could still be alive and dealing with what was going on.

In December of 1966, Mae celebrated the best Christmas she would have with her children. Although there were no gifts or anything of

monetary value bought or exchanged, she was
thankful for the children that had been returned
to her.

First Christmas after the rebellion
and two years of being in the forest

THE REBUILDING

Mae was now starting over again. With everything left behind in Kalanganda from the result of the rebellion, Mae turned to a non-profit organization that was established around the time the Congo got its independence. It was called CPRA (Congo Protestant Relief Agency), based out of Matadi. The CPRA was formed by US missionaries to aid other missionaries working with schools and hospitals around the Congo. There was a young gentleman named Timothy Lind who worked at the CPRA office representing the Mennonite church. Tim was of great assistance to Mae and the orphanage. She would request their assistance once a month with supplies, such as food, clothing, shoes, blankets, etc.

Tim would accommodate Mae's request for supplies at no cost. Meanwhile, as Mae dealt with the children's physical and emotional healing, she was also concerned about her new surroundings. The old vacant store where she was living was in an old commercial district area called Kitambo. It was not the best area of town. It was only a couple blocks away from a rough area where some gangs were known to frequent. There were instances of violence and robberies that they heard about. The inner city reflected some of the chaos and turmoil that was happening in the country in general.

Mae and the orphans were not used to city life. Furthermore, Mae felt called and fulfilled working in the villages with the indigenous people, living a simpler life. She wasn't sure she would be able to adapt to the city life and where God was now calling her to. She would be open to wherever the Lord would send her to! The overpopulated area, along with the lack of structure within the community, made for an unstable environment. This was all foreign to Mae and the children.

There was continued fighting in different parts of the Congo that included Congolese military personnel and rebels that stemmed from continued foreign influence. In the village where Mae and the children used to live, they had structured leadership starting with the chiefs, who carried out the disciplinary actions in the community, and close-knit families, which held their children and relatives responsible for any actions which caused embarrassment to their families. The locals were very respectful, and they were proud of who they were and the traditions they had, and they worked together well.

Mae found city life continuously challenging, especially when she encountered an attempt to break into the store a few weeks after moving in. A few months later, another incident occurred. Some of the older boys who had come back from the rebellion had some run-ins with other neighborhood boys. Mae was really concerned, and she remembered meeting some UN and military officials when she returned to the city while she was waiting to hear any news about her missing children. One of the officials she met was named Kitoko.

He was a Christian and wanted to help Mae in any way that he could if she needed his assistance. Mae decided to call on him to help her in dealing with the crime and violence. Kitoko was more than happy to help. He worked at a military base not too far from where Mae and the kids lived. He would come around and also send some of his personnel to make the occasional appearance at the house. Kitoko would later become an army chaplain, and he would continue the close relationship he had with Mae and the kids of the orphanage for the next several years. As Mae continued living in the city, more and more problems arose. But there were still children to love and care for and souls to be saved. Mae and the orphan children attended the local church on Sundays.

Kitoko with his family at
the orphanage

She took in a lot more children in the next two years and now had twenty-four kids in total. Mae was also provided with a new van to get around in the city. The old van was destroyed with the old compound in Kalanganda during the rebellion. Mae missed the village life as far as community cooperation and the slower pace. As Mae and the children outgrew the temporary store, she heard about a two-acre property in the outskirts of the capital, which was called Makanpan. It was a large area that other companies also wanted. Not only that, but the surrounding businesses began to put pressure on the government because they also wanted the same piece of land. Mae began to pray about how to get the land and how she would pay for it.

Mae did not have much hope that the government would help her since Mobutu, then president for a couple of years, had complete power over land and properties. He had changed the names of historic places that had been appointed in colonial times as a way to show his dominance. One of these name changes would be the capital city of Leopoldville, which was now called Kinshasa. The president was attempting to bring on a spirit of nationalism and unity to the Congo. Mae welcomed it, knowing that the Congolese people needed and deserved it after years of violence and oppression.

Mae wasn't convinced, however, that Mobutu should have been the person to usher it into the newly independent Congo. She didn't approve of him asserting himself as president in the way of a coup, then canceling elections right after that, supposedly for the next five years. Mae believed that the former president (Joseph Kasavubu), who went to a missionary school as a young boy and had a desire for ministry while attending seminary for a short period preceding his role as president of Congo, had more moral values. Mae also disapproved when President Mobutu dismissed the former Prime Minister Moise Tchombe, with whom Mae had a respectful and professional relationship. Tchombe was also taught good moral values as a young boy while attending missionary school.

A few months later, Mae received a letter from her youngest sister, Alma. She informed Mae that their dad had passed away. Mae was devastated by the news, and in 1968, she asked Marie if she could stay at the orphanage while she took a six-week furlough back to the States. Mae took a much-needed six-week furlough. She was able to see her family and friends, who were happy to see her alive since they had read in her letters about the rebellion and all the hardships and challenges that she was faced with. She visited her family in Pennsylvania and Maryland, and she also went to Akron, Ohio, to the church that was helping to support her.

While she was in the States in the fall of 1968, she was surprised to see and hear about all the turmoil that the US had gone through that year. Mae was saddened to hear about the assassination of Reverend Martin Luther King Jr. earlier that year in April. She believed that he was a man of God and a good leader for the Black community. He was also a voice for the oppressed and the poor in this country and a symbol of inspiration for those who were exploited around the world. Mae felt that it was moving away from the principles of God. The country seemed divided by the Vietnam War, and there were other signs that it was heading in the wrong direction.

This was not the US she once knew and loved. Mae had been away for more than twenty years and, despite her extraordinary challenges and accomplishments, had tried her best to keep engaged in the complexities and events that took place in the US for the past quarter of a century. She still hoped and believed that the America she once knew and had left would still continue to be the vehicle and instrument that God would use to proclaim the Gospel of Christ to the world. Mae always believed, especially through experience, that difficulty brought people to prayer and back to God, and the desire for God's intervention was desperately needed and hopefully welcomed.

Mae was glad to see her family and some of her old friends again. She did not realize it then, but it would be the last time she would see all but one sister and brother. The rest of her siblings would have passed away by the next time she returned to the States. On September 25th, 1968, Mae's dad died from heart failure. She was able to be there for the funeral, but it was a bittersweet gathering. He was buried in Greenville, PA, next to his wife. She was sad that her dad had passed away but happy he was saved and with the Lord. Mae reflected back on some of her own health issues, including her heart murmurs, diabetes, and just her overall well-being.

As much as she enjoyed being home and seeing her family, she had to get back to the Congo. As she flew back, she reflected on her years in the Congo. She started to wonder what the future held for her. She had seen progress, setbacks, and change in the Congo these past three decades. What changes would she face now?

THE REVIVAL

A couple of months after returning to the Congo, Mae saw the closest thing to a revival that she could have imagined. There was an evangelist named T. L. Osborn who toured the continent of Africa. Dr. T. L. Osborn was a missionary and evangelist who had been proclaiming the Gospel of Jesus Christ in many different countries. In 1969, he went to the Congo for a week. He held his crusade in the stadium of Kinshasa, and Mae decided to take the children. Mae took the kids who wanted to go in the new Volkswagen van, and some missionary friends took the other kids that didn't fit in the van.

Evangelist Osborn had an exciting and charismatic personality. Mae and the children enjoyed their time listening to the worship music and the preaching at the crusade. After the crusade was over, everyone seemed to be in high spirits. Mae felt that, after three decades in the Congo, the week-long revival had been much overdue. Mae was very excited that the orphan children experienced a crusade of this magnitude. Possibly a once in a lifetime experience for them!

Just as the experience of the crusade began to fade, more details about the property in Makanpan became available. The two-acre property available for purchase had been promised by the prime minister a couple of years before. It was on an undeveloped side of Kinshasa, in an area called Macampagne. Since it had been two years, Mae was not sure if the government would honor their agreement because there were now different members in the government.

Mae had only been promised the availability of the land for purchase, but she had to come up with the finances herself. So she once again began praying for a miracle from God. She went down to the government's office and inquired about the property that had been promised to her. Unfortunately, no one had any recollection of it.

As she was about to leave, a lady came up to her whom she recognized. It was Marguerite, the same lady she had spoken to the time before. She remembered Mae and remembered the promise that was made to her. Marguerite assured Mae that the promise would be honored. After nine months had passed, two church leaders named John Claude and Malcom McVeigh, associated with the MCC

(Mennonite Central Committee) Church World Service, went to see her and gave her a check for three thousand dollars from the organization to buy the land for the new orphanage.

Tim Lind, representing the Mennonite church, was the overseer for the building of the orphanage. Tim would come by the construction site every day and report back the progress that was being made. Part of having a new orphanage also included having a new board. The board consisted of nine members, mostly Christian, Congolese businessmen, and pastors. Mae continued to send out newsletters in the Congo and to the States since now, more than ever, she needed the support. Later, the Congo Gospel Mission would also contribute with funds.

The orphanage was named the Rutherford Memorial Orphanage. The land was located at 3374 Ave. Ring in Zone Ngaliema Macampagne, and it was purchased in 1968. Mae was named treasurer and partial owner. She would be given the freedom to run the orphanage as she saw fit but now had to come up with the funds to build the orphanage. The plans included a large building that consisted of two large dormitories, one for the boys and one for the girls. It also included two bathrooms in each of the dormitories, a large dining room, a living room area, and a kitchen. The plans included a separate bedroom and bathroom for Mae. The perimeter would have a concrete wall surrounding the three-acre compound. Each wing would need to be large enough to house thirteen beds each for a maximum capacity of twenty-six orphans.

Mae continued sending out newsletters, asking for support, and little by little, contributions started to trickle in. So much so that she was able to start building the orphanage. Her prayers had been answered, and she was so thankful to all of those that had helped her! While the orphanage was being built, the older orphan kids would go after school and on Saturdays to help out on the construction site. The boys and girls would remove weeds, stones, trash and do any other small task that they could help with. Two of the older boys assisted the hired masons working on the construction.

Mae kept in contact with the nine board members, and one of them was Pastor Dhanis, whom she had been friends with for ten years and had helped her search for the children that were rescued after the rebellion. Another board member was Pastor Joseph, who had a large church compared to most others in the area. This was the church where Mae and her orphan children would attend and call their home church. Another member was Pastor Andre, whom Mae had mentored previously. He was a young man who would visit periodically and help facilitate different projects concerning the orphanage.

It took another year before the facility was finished. Finally, in 1969, Mae and her orphan children moved into the new compound. The property, which was several acres of land, accommodated Mae and the orphans well. Mae continued to write newsletters asking those in Africa and the United States for prayer and financial support for the orphanage.

There was still concern about violence and crime in the area where the new orphanage was, and Kitoko continued to provide protection for Mae as he had done so previously in Kintambo. When Mae visited the military camp to see Kitoko, she would take the opportunity to share the Gospel and give Bibles to the soldiers. She knew that soldiers' lives were stressful and could come to an end at any time. Therefore, she always felt an urgency to share the Gospel with them.

Soldiers that Mae shared the
Gospel with

A make-shift soccer field was the major form of
entertainment for the boys. They played a couple
of times a week after dinner. Mae and the children
also enjoyed evening devotionals, which consisted of
singing, reading, sharing, and prayer. The chores had
to be done before the devotional, which was the last
event before bedtime. The chores consisted of not

only cleaning up after dinner but also tending to the domestic animals, like rabbits, chickens, goats, a monkey named JoJo, and two dogs named Sparkle and Fanny. There was also a vegetable garden in the back of the property that needed to be taken care of.

Mae's helpers in Kalanganda did not follow her to the city since they all had families of their own. She had to find new helpers in the city. Mae took in seven more children while in the city, for a total of twenty-three. Gaston, one of the oldest orphans, took over the role of cooking and helping with the vegetable garden. Mae used the new van to go to the market, church, and to go to the hospital or the doctor's office. The new van served the orphanage well for getting around in the city.

All the orphan children walked to school every day, which was a few blocks from their home. The children spoke Kikongo and Lingala. They also learned French, and some of them caught on to it well enough to be able to speak it on the street. There were French words that were common to the everyday Congolese citizen, especially since the country's national anthem was in French. All the kids were expected to be in church every Sunday, and the older ones were encouraged to be involved in choir or youth activities. This was not hard since the church was only a couple of blocks away.

The new Volkswagen van with some of the kids along the side

All of the children also spoke English since Mae would mainly speak that at home. Two of the orphan boys went to an English-speaking foreign school (TASOK) for a couple of years. It was a foreign school open to all kids starting from kindergarten through high school. Mae spoke English and Kikongo, and she knew a little bit of Lingala and a couple of words in French too. French was being taught more and more each day in all the schools. People in the government, universities, and professionals spoke mostly French, but for the average Congolese, it was still not part of their culture.

Mae received two volunteers to help out in the orphanage, which she really welcomed. One was a forty-year-old paraplegic man who loved children. His name was Ebala. He would come and help out whenever he could, give emotional support, and teach the children important life values. He had a great sense of humor and had a positive influence on the children. Another helper, who the children would call "Mama" Ester, was a local lady who would come now and then to help with the cooking and cleaning. One of the older boys and two of the older girls would also help out with the cooking. Rice, beans, and meat from the market or chickens raised on the property would provide for the everyday meal, along with vegetables from the garden that was on the premises. Rice and flour would be stored away for year-round use. One of the favorite meals served was fufu, which was made from manioc flour that was poured into a huge pot of boiling water. This would be served with saka saka, makayabu (dried fish) and bitekuteku.

The children had to walk to and from school every day and finish their chores when they got home. Some of the older teenage boys ran into trouble with some gang members and ended up spending a couple of days in jail. The jails in the city were very rough places to be in. When they got out, they came back home with bumps and bruises and definitely learned their lesson the hard way. As the children got older and wanted to be more independent, they began to go outside of the orphanage and work and learn trades. Some got married and started families of their own.

In September of 1971, Mae received a four-year-old girl named Amina. She needed special attention because she had polio and wore braces on both legs. She could hardly walk without help. She was a very quiet, cute little girl. There was always room for one more child. Mae took in different types of children; most of them were children or babies who were considered cursed, whose mother had died in childbirth. But on occasion, she received older children with physical or mental disabilities. Mae also took in siblings because she felt it would not be right to separate them since it was hard enough without their parents there. Babies would come to

Mae malnourished and dehydrated, which required lots of care, and some also needed special medicine. She spent many months taking care of them and nursing them back to health. At other times, Mae took babies that were deathly ill. But she could not save or take care of all the babies that came to her; she had to turn some away.

The youngest children in the orphanage

One day, as Mae entered her Volkswagen, she reached to close the door, fell, and cut her arm on an open tin can. She didn't think much of it but eventually had to get a tetanus shot. She had to wear a sling since she also fractured her arm in the fall. This was one of the many injuries that Mae sustained while she was in the Congo. But no matter how busy Mae was throughout the day or what injuries she had, she would always make time for the evening devotions with all of the children.

Mae had established a good relationship with the community in Kinshasa, and it was a successful transition from the village to the city. She felt the orphanage was established and progressing now, even though it had been an adjustment from village life. She would come to know a variety of people, including local pastors that she worked with, along with businessmen, teachers, politicians, military personnel, and common citizens in the neighborhood and communities. Mae was also well respected and admired by all of those who encountered her. The children were also expected to be a good example, whether in Sunday school or in the school classroom and in the community. She expected this from the youngest to the oldest in her orphanage and did not exclude those who were older, even those in their twenties, and had already moved out on their own.

Mae continued to raise her children with discipline and love. She knew that living in the city would bring different challenges of its own, different from village life. Some said that Mae was much stricter in the early years with the children, especially with the girls, and she always expected her children to demonstrate good qualities and set a good example as missionary kids. Mae continued to be concerned with the older children since she knew the consequences of teenage delinquency had negative implications for her boys. If they continued hanging with the wrong crowd, they could go to jail again or even receive serious beatings if the military police saw fit. The orphan kids learned to see that Mae's way of discipline was for a good reason and that it wasn't as strict compared to the outside authority.

One day, her good friend Kitoko told her about the current president Mobutu and what was going on. Mae was somewhat aware of some of the things since other missionaries had mentioned them to her. There were rumors about

the president imprisoning and exterminating
individuals opposing his regime and his political
party. It seemed that the dictator was content with
the people as long as no one dared to speak out
against him. The young people, especially those
that were informed and educated, were bold enough
to speak out against the regime. This was especially
prominent at the universities.

It all came to a climax when Mobutu became
irritated enough that he sent the military
to the university to put an end to the public
demonstrations. The military went to the university
and opened fire on students, therefore, killing
several. Then, he continued by shutting down the
university and mandated the rest of the students to
join the military in order to be indoctrinated to his
beliefs. But there were citizens who were content
with the apparent peace and prosperity, along with
the stability that seemed to be in the country, and
who were tired of all the violence that preceded the
whole first half of the century. Other demonstrators
across the country would come to the same demise.
The dictator also decided to put himself at the head
of the church, vowing to replace Christianity. This
idea did not sit well with Mae and the other pastors

and missionaries. There were also other citizens and many foreigners that showed concern with the dictator's behavior.

Mae was one of the people that was aware and concerned with his actions. It seemed that he was trying to create a cult for himself. With the events that had been transpiring in the Congo, along with concerns about her own health, Mae began to contemplate the future of the orphanage. She mentioned her concern to the board members, and they said they would support whatever decision she felt she needed to make.

THE DICTATOR

Before 1960, Joseph Desiree Mobutu was a sergeant major in the military, which was the highest rank open to the Congolese in the colonized country. In 1960, the Congo got its independence from Belgium, and Mobutu promoted himself to commander in chief of the military. Joseph Kasavubu became president, and Patrice Lumumba became the prime minister. Mobutu, consequently, became secretary of state in late 1960 and then accused Lumumba of being a communist sympathizer. Soon after, the Congolese soldiers rebelled against the White Belgium officers, and Belgium flew more troops in to take control of the situation.

Lumumba interpreted this move as a threat to the independence of the Congo and asked for help from the UN and the United States. When they refused, Lumumba asked the Soviet Union for help. Belgium and the Western allies backed Mobutu, resulting in Prime Minister Lumumba being removed from office in December of 1960 and executed in January of 1961. This resulted in Mobutu becoming the commander of the military forces and sharing equal leadership with President

Kasavubu. In November of 1965, there was a military coup in which President Kasavubu was ousted and sent into exile by Mobutu.

He, then, declared himself president, denouncing any other rivals. In 1965, he would change the country's name again from the Republic of Congo to the Democratic Republic of Congo. The second prime minister of the Congo, Moise Tshombe, was also eventually ousted and sent into exile by Mobutu. He would now be the only state official and representative in the DRC. In 1967, President Mobutu established a party called MPR, which stood for Movement of the Popular Revolution. The MPR party did not recognize any other party. In 1970, his single party would become a constitutional law, and Mobutu would make his government look like a democratic pro-election society to the outside world and not require any aid from foreign countries. The MPR would control the Secret Service, which was part of Mobutu's regime, and would execute rival leaders and others that threatened his regime, along with imprisoning any citizens that spoke out against the dictator.

A few months had passed when Mobutu changed his name to Mobutu Sese Seko, meaning "the all-powerful warrior" in Lingala. Mae, and many other citizens, felt the name change was eventually the start of him thinking of himself as some sort of deity. Mobutu insisted and reveled in everyone around him calling and treating him as a god they should worship. The citizens felt threatened if they did not participate in the rhetoric, and this worship would be encouraged through propaganda and media. Mobutu was careful not to call himself "god" in public but would encourage the minister of propaganda to proclaim his deity to the nation. Mobutu's songs had lyrics such as "Mobutu, our god lord, and creator, protector of our country."

The media would portray Mobutu's picture and show clouds all around, giving the image that he was a god that came out of the clouds. Congolese children in school would be told that Mobutu was a god and that he should be worshiped. Many obeyed and believed what they were taught. Hearing everything that the pastors and the military chaplain presented to her, Mae did not want to think about leaving the children for any reason, no matter how dangerous it became.

Shortly after, Mae began to experience some

symptoms of her physical ailments. She was now sixty years old, and some of her family's health history seemed to be catching up with her. She now had heart issues, which needed to be addressed by her American doctors. She knew that, in the last decade, some of her family members had passed away from heart issues. The doctor told her that she needed to pace herself. He told her, *"If you only had a couple of children to raise, then that would be manageable and reasonable, but with twenty-two children, how is that even possible?"* Mae laughed at his comment.

At the beginning of 1971, President Mobutu changed the country's name for the third time, from the Republic of the Congo to Zaire. He also began to amass a financial fortune through financial exploitation and corruption. There were rumors circulating that Mobutu was talking about taking over the foreign companies in Zaire and seizing them for himself and other fellow loyalists. Things got economically worse for the Congolese people. Religious establishments also became a target, which Mae thought would affect the orphanage. This led Americans and Europeans to start leaving the country.

Mae was encouraged by missionary friends

and the board of her orphanage to leave in order
to receive better healthcare and to make an early
attempt to put the orphan children back into their
villages before it was too late. The board felt that,
at any time, the religious organizations could be
seized by the government. Mae refused to leave the
kids a second time; her hesitance was because she
felt that if she had stayed the first time during the
rebellion, then her sixteen children that died would
have survived. Also, this time around, it was not a
civil war.

In 1972, Mobutu made an order declaring all
citizens to drop their Christian names and use
their Africanized names only. Mae would hope that
the Lord would change the dictator somehow. She
was disappointed in how everything was changing
since it seemed it was for the worse. But this wasn't
the only turmoil that was going on in the world.
The United States was still in a war with Vietnam.
Things seemed to be unstable everywhere. Mae,
through the years, had to leave the Congo at times
but felt positive because it was only for a temporary
period of time. This time, it felt more permanent.
Mae considered leaving the orphanage for Mary to
look after, but possibly on just a temporary basis

until things were better. Mary lived in a village hours away, so Mae sent her a letter explaining her dilemma and asking if she wanted to take over the orphanage on a temporary basis.

She thought if circumstances changed for the best, then she could return to the Congo, and if they didn't, then she would discuss with Mary a possible permanent situation. Mae began to make plans to go back to the States. She knew the longer she waited, the more difficult it would be for the children to be placed if Mary decided not to take over for her. She needed to start looking right away so she could have more time to carefully place the children. She didn't hear back from Mary, so she began to work on placements for the children. For the next period of a few months, she would grudgingly and painfully place her children in the care of others. Most of them would go back to their villages to live with their relatives.

PREPARING TO LEAVE

Mae knew, deep inside her heart, that this decision would alter the course of her and the children's lives. She had no choice but to leave for health and safety reasons. She was considering taking only two children back with her to the States. The thought of bringing only two children back out of the twenty-four with her was a very difficult and painful one. She wished that she was able to take all twenty-four children with her, but that was an extreme impossibility. Even if she could get documents for all of them, there was no way she could support them financially. Some of the orphan kids that were over eighteen and had jobs and the help of missionary friends could survive on their own, but the rest could not. Mae lived month to month in the Congo, and she had enough to only buy her airline tickets, but not much more than that. The church support would help take care of those needs each time.

The thought of taking two of the children with her still lingered in her heart, and she mentioned it to the board of directors. They said that the government had strict rules against that.

She asked what she could do about it. They said they did not think she could do much about it. Mae prayed about the matter, and she knew the Lord would need to provide a way. She decided to go down to the government office anyway to talk to them about the possibility of doing so.

When Mae went to the state department and asked about taking two children back to the States with her, the lady told her that the only way was through adoption. Even though she had raised her children from birth, the only way to take them with her was to officially adopt them. Although there was a lot of red tape with the regulations, she was happy that there was an avenue through adoption. Mae asked how long the process would take and said that she wanted to leave for the States in six months or so. The lady said that would be impossible to accomplish. She still pursued the process and trusted the Lord about it.

She began the process of adoption with Bobby and Teddy while dealing with the other situations concerning the other children and the crisis that was happening in the country. Mae got in contact with the gentleman who had been referred to her at the state department. The gentleman said things were crazy, paperwork was backed up, and that the process was slow and could take up to a year or more. He was polite and cooperative with Mae. She knew that she didn't want to wait a year or longer to leave the Congo for the States, but if it was the only way to legally take the two children with her, then she would leave it in the Lord's hands and His timing on when to leave.

She figured she had about nine months to get the kids situated in a place where they would be safe. Mae tried to place the children into other missions, but she didn't get very far. The country was not stable, and she knew that there wouldn't be any place that would be exempt from the turmoil. A month or so had passed, and Mae had not heard back from Mary about taking over the orphanage. Mae didn't know why Mary hadn't responded, but she had to make decisions regardless. She had also asked Marie if she was willing to stay at the orphanage but knew Marie was committed to her own mission. Plus, Marie had told her previously that she was also contemplating returning to the States since she too had her health issues to think about.

Mae cried and prayed every night in anguish for the children. She prayed that there would somehow be an escape from this difficult decision. She realized that her only hope was to send the children back to the relatives in the villages that they had come from. Hopefully, the relatives would take them in and come together to take care of them. Within two months, Mae received a letter from the gentleman at the government office, who stated that he did not know how it happened, but the adoption papers had been processed, and the adoption would be finalized any day. Mae was relieved and felt God opening doors.

As it was getting closer to her departure, Mae placed the last children in their prospective villages. Thankfully most of them were older children that were independent and could manage on their own. It was hard to say goodbye to each and every one of them, but she did. She left the orphanage building in the trust of the board members and also wrote them a letter making them aware of her request for Mary, her first and oldest orphan, to run the orphanage, possibly in a temporary or permanent capacity.

The last picture of Mae's children
taken in the orphanage before it
closed for good in 1972

Mae had no idea where she would live once she
was back in the States. She had no home to go to
with her adopted children. She had written letters
a couple of months before to several friends, all
over the US, asking for a place to stay until she
could get back on her feet, but she had not received
any replies. Finally, a couple of weeks before her
departure for the US, she received a letter from an
old friend named Wilma Linkie. She was one of

Mae's roommates from Royalton, Kentucky, where they did full-time ministry together.

Wilma was living by herself and was partially blind at the time. She had settled herself for a few years now in Beaumont, California. Mae had made contact with her periodically throughout the years. Wilma offered Mae a place to stay, and Mae accepted her offer. She had never been to California before. In fact, Mae had never been anywhere near the West Coast region of the United States. She had only lived and traveled in the eastern and midwestern parts of the country.

She now had a place to go to, along with her two kids that she had adopted, thirteen-year-old Bobby and seven-year-old Teddy. As Mae got ready for her departure, she started to wonder if she would ever see the kids who would stay behind or if she would ever see the Congo again. She already missed her home. She always thought that she would remain permanently in the Congo until her death. She thought she was going to be able to live there and die there. This was the second most painful day of her life, the first being when she found out that some of her children had been killed in the rebellion. She started to wonder if this

had all been in vain. Did she make a difference?
Was this how it was all going to turn out after
everything was said and done?

BACK TO THE US

At the age of sixty-two, after almost twenty-seven years of being in the Congo, Mae moved back to the States. Mae and her two children moved to California in the spring of 1972. When she first arrived in the US, she visited her family in Pennsylvania, Maryland, and Ohio. Most of the family that she visited were Christians, which she was pleased about. She only had three siblings that were still alive, a younger sister and two younger brothers. After visiting back east, they flew out west and settled in California.

Mae continued to keep in contact with her children who stayed in the Congo through missionary friends who were still there, along with communicating with the older adult children. She continued to struggle with the decision to leave the Congo, even though the reasons were valid. Mae had heart issues, high blood pressure, and borderline diabetes. She could seek care for those issues now that she was living in the US.

Mae lived in Beaumont, California, for a year, while Bobby and Teddy attended public school in the area. In 1973, Mae heard that Mobutu's dictatorship government had seized foreign companies and organizations. She also heard that her orphanage had been seized and sold. She was not sure how that really could have happened since she was part owner. She was aware of the corruption that had been happening but didn't realize it was this blatant. The board members wrote Mae to keep her informed and said they would see what they could do to fight the illegal sale of the property.

She also found out, by corresponding back and forth with friends, that Mary had never received the letter that she sent to her asking if she was willing to manage the orphanage. Mary articulated her sorrow to Mae and stated that she definitely would have accepted that permanent or temporary role at the orphanage. Mae and Marie had also been corresponding back and forth because Mae had a desire to get more of her children to the States if possible. Marie said she would do what she could.

For the next year, they worked on getting more of the orphan kids to the States. By 1974, Mae would be joined by her best friend Marie, who brought over three additional orphans on temporary visas. Marie stated that things were getting worse in the Congo as far as poverty and corruption. Marie stayed in California only for a short stay before returning to the eastern part of the United States to live there. Three more children would come to stay with her within the next two years. Mae now had five of her kids living in California with her: Gaston, Ronny, Bobby, Dale, and Teddy.

Even after Mae was able to bring more of her children to the States, she was still not content with the situation of the orphanage. She was still worried about the effects the other children had been exposed to with the civil unrest and the dictatorship tactics that were going on. Mae continued to correspond with the board members and hoped one day to return when it was safer so she could fight to retrieve the orphanage. She was hopeful that somehow she could get help from the US in dealing with the situation back in the Congo on the seizing of foreigners' lands and businesses. Mae thought that, in time, the US might look into all the issues of injustice happening in the Congo. But she knew that it would probably not even be on their radar since Vietnam and the Nixon impeachment situation were taking place.

Mae and her boys back in the
States in 1974

Since Mae received more orphan children from the Congo, she began to focus on getting a bigger place to live. She knew there was not enough room for her and all the children living with her old friend Wilma. After looking for some time, she found a place in Ontario for her and the children to move into. She was grateful for her good friend from Kentucky for opening her house in Beaumont to her and her family, as inconvenient as it might have been for her. Mae continued to receive financial support from churches and friends. She also continued with her daily nightly devotions with the kids as she had done in the Congo.

Even though instead of twenty-something kids, now it would be with just a few. Given that the younger kids were in school, the older kids, who were over eighteen years of age, would find jobs while continuing their education. Mae felt a strong desire to send the three youngest children, Bobby, Dale, and Teddy, to a private school. She had no idea where or how that was going to come about financially, especially in a new location. She started looking in the yellow pages and began calling around to different places. She finally received a call back from a small private school. The principal and his family came out to interview Mae and her family. The name of the principal was Ed Dial, and his wife Taylora, who was a teacher at the private school.

The school was called Calvary Baptist and was located in La Verne, California. Ed and Taylora would accommodate Mae and her children as much as possible to make things work for her family. The school was not set up for foreign students, but Ed and Taylora were willing to help out with the immigration guidelines in order to pass the requirements necessary to get the children ready and able to attend their school. The school was part of Calvary Baptist Church, whose pastors were Dr. and Mrs. S. T. Sullivan, also known as Pastor Taylor and Jean Sullivan. They were the parents of Taylora, the principal's wife. The church and the school opened their arms out to help so that Teddy, Dale, and Bobby could attend the private school.

The school was very accommodating to all different types of families, including children from low-income families and with special needs. Mae and her children felt comfortable and accepted there. Mae worked in the school cafeteria, and the children qualified for partial financial aid to attend. The three children also contributed toward working off some of their tuition by doing after-school tasks such as emptying classroom trash and picking up trash on the school grounds. Ed and Taylora would become mentors to Mae's children that attended the school. They would play an important and influential role long after their school-age years were done. Later on, Mae would enroll Teddy at Western Christian High School. The administration there was also very accommodating with Mae's financial circumstances.

Another mentor for the boys at the school was a coach and teacher named Chappy. He would be like a big brother to the boys, and he was also Taylora's younger brother. Mae would also begin a close relationship with Erma Jackson, who was the pastor's mother-in-law. Everyone called her Mawmaw Jackson. The pastor's family would embrace Mae's family as much as any family could. Mae would also continue to receive some support from organizations, though it had decreased since she returned back to the States. Goss Memorial Church in Akron, Ohio, which first pledged to support Mae when she first worked in the Appalachian Mountains in the early nineteen-thirties, would be one of the few that would continue their financial support.

Some people said that Mae wasn't retired, even though she did not have an orphanage anymore. This was because she still had some of her orphan children that she brought over from the Congo. Another reason was that Mae also became involved in an organization called the David Livingston Missionary Foundation. She was interested in an organization that a missionary and an abolitionist such as David Livingston would be connected to. It was an international organization that sponsored orphans around the world. Mae decided to financially sponsor two orphans, one in Korea and one in India. She started the financial support in 1974 and planned to continue the support for many years to come. She had an entire picture album filled and dedicated to one of her orphan kids from South Korea named Chung Soon Kim. She also decided to sponsor an orphan from an organization called Compassion International. The orphan child was from India, and his name was Ganta Jesuratnam. Mae also planned to sponsor him until the sponsorship limit age of eighteen.

Mae continued to be very involved in her church and in the community. She became a faithful lifetime member at her church in La Verne. She was also supportive of missions by mentioning them whenever she spoke at public events. She was the lifeline and the heartbeat of the mission's outreach in her community. Because of her vision and understanding, she brought those around her to a higher level of responsibility. Mae was a powerful prayer warrior who also led the prayer ministry at her church. In the community, Mae had speaking engagements at colleges, town halls, and churches through the next several decades. She would bring along with her an old projector that allowed her to show still slides and motion picture slides from the early years in the US and in the Congo. It was part of her presentation that she enjoyed sharing, whether it was with a captive audience or just a single friend.

She was the neighborhood mom who would invite children, including parents, and share what she could, whether it was food, advice, or spiritual guidance. She would break out a flannel graph board like she had done so many times before in the Congo, with props and Bible characters for a nice visual, and she would tell Bible stories to the neighborhood kids who would be over at the time or previously invited specifically for this purpose.

Mae would tell Teddy to invite all the neighborhood kids to the house Bible storytime. This happened more often in the summertime when kids were out on break, but on occasions, Mae would have a Saturday afternoon Bible storytime during the regular school year. She usually put cookies and punch out for those who wanted to snack on something afterward. Mae also gave those in the church and the community an awareness and an eagerness to become more accountable to God with their lives. She mentored and influenced women of all ages in the church and community in many ways.

In 1975, after a couple of years of living in Ontario, and with the help of those still supporting her, she was able to purchase a bigger house in Claremont, CA, which accommodated her and her five children. It was a nice community for her and the children to reside in. Soon after, the kids made friends in the neighborhood. Mae met a neighbor down the street named Opal, and both families would celebrate birthdays and holidays together. Mae became a spiritual mentor to Opal, who was about ten years younger than her. Opal came to admire Mae's life journey and character as their friendship became close and she learned more about her life. The private school that Mae's children attended had now established a foreign student exchange program and, therefore, would have a consistent flow of foreign students from around the world. Eventually, the three older kids would move out on their own. The youngest two were still at home and attending private school.

Dale, the second youngest, was sixteen years of age and was involved with different organized sports, including football and basketball, along with community soccer.

One summer day, Dale came home in the afternoon from playing soccer in the park, and his behavior was very abnormal. Mae was very concerned and didn't know what to do. Dale became paranoid, thinking people were after him, and began to hallucinate, claiming that he was burning up from being set on fire. He also displayed other abnormal behavioral symptoms. Mae thought maybe Dale had taken some type of drug or that he was given some sort of substance by his peers while at the park. She took Dale to the hospital, but no substance was found. The behavior continued for the next several days, and Dale was taken to different clinics. One of the doctors at the clinic diagnosed him as suffering from some type of mental disorder.

Dale's behavior became harmful, not to those around him, but more so concerning his own well-being. He began to show behaviors such as banging his head against the wall or being frightened to the extent of having a panic attack. Because Mae felt he could be a danger to himself, she decided that it would be best for all to have him permanently hospitalized. He was institutionalized at Camarillo State Hospital. Mae attributed the breakdown to possibly all of the traumatic stress he had endured as a child while in the Congo during the rebellion. Dale was about four years of age and one of the youngest kids in the orphanage, running and hiding with other refugees in the forest. While in the forest, he ran away from soldiers and wild animals while facing starvation. This diagnosis would change his future and affect the rest of the family. The entire family would go and visit Dale periodically. He resided at the state hospital for a year until he received the right medication that controlled his behavior. He was taken out of the state hospital and put into a group home that was managed by the State. The family would continue to be supportive of Dale and interact with him by bringing him home and involving him in the family events as much as possible throughout the years to come. Mae would always have a special place in her heart for Dale.

Mae's other orphan children were also still dealing with the psychological and emotional effects of having been refugee children in the middle of a war zone in the Congo. Self-confidence, survivor's guilt, along with recurring nightmares would be part of the challenges some of the other children still faced. Mae tried to be supportive and encouraging to them, but it was still difficult dealing with the trauma. She had missionary and Christian friends who encouraged her as she continued to be a support to them.

THE FIGHT FOR
THE ORPHANAGE

In 1981, at the age of seventy-one, Mae decided that it was time to attempt a trip to the Congo. She still had not given up on regaining ownership of the orphanage from the government that had taken it from her. After nine years of being away, Mae landed in the country where at one time, she thought she would live out the rest of her life. Mae stayed at a missionary Baptist location where she met up with Mary after writing that she was coming. Mae remembered how it was when she first landed in the Congo in 1946 and how so many things had changed since then.

By the end of the week, Mae had seen and heard about how much worse the Congo was since she left close to a decade ago. The poverty level was much worse in the country, and Mobutu had continued to keep the country repressed. There had been several failed coup attempts, which resulted in more imprisonments and executions of the opposition. He was also married to more than one wife, which didn't sit well with missionaries and pastors either. The first few years that

Mobutu was president created some stability and some prosperity for the people. The first years of his rule seemed to be promising at that time, but now he had shown his true colors and set the Congolese people back to how it was before their independence. Mae was informed, by her missionary friends, that corruption was rampant everywhere; the infrastructure had collapsed, and schools, hospitals, and roads had deteriorated. The living conditions had turned unbearable.

Mae's worst fears were confirmed on her first trip back after moving to the States. Mae believed that when anyone puts themselves as the head of the church and demands that the country worship them as god instead of the one true God, that country is headed for disaster no matter how stable the country seems to be at the time. After being there a week, Mae requested and was granted an appointment with the current prime minister at the time, who was Nguza Karl I Bond. In early 1981, Mae met and presented her case while he listened. He stated that he would look into the matter and get back to her. Meanwhile, Mae made an attempt to locate some of the orphan children that had stayed.

When she spoke with friends and some of the orphan children, she found out more information about the orphanage that was very disturbing. One of the orphan children named Gideon, who was now a grown man, had sided with the corrupt government. He lied about the orphanage building and created false documents while undermining everything Mae had tried to do with the orphanage compound. He had been an insider that Mae had not counted on to outwardly denounce the orphanage and make threats to those who were associated with the orphanage. Some of the children became fearful of him, while others stood up and would not associate with him because he had the backing of some of the corrupt leaders. Mae was also told that Gideon had threatened her life if she tried to come back and fight for the orphanage. Once Gideon's wife caught on with what Gideon had been doing, she opposed his actions. Her response to Gideon resulted in her mysterious death soon after.

Mae was shocked and saddened but understood the corruption in the Congo. It was an ongoing theme in this war-torn country. She heard back from the prime minister, but it wasn't the news she wanted to hear. He stated that there was really nothing he could do. After spending another week seeing her orphan children, Mae was ready to go back to the States. She knew that, unless the dictator, who was brutal and had terrorized the country and eliminated enemies and those who spoke out against him, was put out of power, the turmoil in the Congo would still remain the same.

Mae returned to the States, where she witnessed the graduation of her youngest kid from high school and her older kids from college. Despite the good things that were happening, she became increasingly concerned with things happening in the country, especially with the US and the Soviet Union threatening each other with a nuclear war. The US had also been talking about a defensive system called "Star Wars." Mae didn't understand the methods to prevent a nuclear war, but she believed and understood that the best means to prevent war would be through the message of the Gospel of Jesus Christ. She believed that it was the responsibility of Christians to spread the Gospel all over the world, including the Soviet Union. Mae also believed that evangelists like Billy Graham and his worldwide crusades were exactly what the world needed to hear.

In 1985, Mae and her youngest child Teddy attended one of his crusades in Anaheim, CA. Teddy signed up to take classes and was there for the week to serve as a counselor at the crusade. Evangelist Billy Graham was not only loved by Christians across many denominational lines but also respected all around the world. He was one of few ministers that crossed racial barriers when it wasn't popular to do so, in the 1950s and '60s, by having crusades that were open to anyone, even though they were supposed to segregate. Reverend Graham was also friends with Dr. Martin Luther King Jr. and had invited him to his crusades to lead in prayer. Mae also admired Corrie ten Boom, whose family saved over eight hundred Jews from Hitler and the Nazi concentration camps. She and her family would be captured and placed in the same Nazi concentration camp that she hid and protected Jewish families from, trying to keep them from being killed. Mae also admired Martin Luther, a protestant reformer who started the protestant church. The late great Dr. Martin Luther King Jr. was named after the protestant reformer. His father, Michael Luther King Sr., changed his name to Martin Luther King Sr. after a trip to Germany and, subsequently, named his son the same.

In 1986, at the age of seventy-six, Mae wanted to make another trip to the Congo, but she did not have the money. With the help of her local church, led by Mae's good friends, Pastor Taylor and Gene Sullivan—whom she had known and been part of their church for the past fourteen years, along with her children—and through the WMA (Women's Missionary Auxiliary), which Mae and all the women of the church were part of, they had a fundraiser to help raise the money to be able to go back to the Congo. This would be her last trip back to the place that she always called home.

Mae went back to the Congo again for about a month. Her main goal was to look into getting the orphanage back. This time, she was escorted by Ronny, one of the eldest children. After they landed at the airport in Kinshasa, Mae could see the change within the people, even from her last visit. Mae also had to be more careful of her surroundings. Workers at the N'Djili Airport were asking for more tips than normal and extra tips if there were two workers. Transportation workers also asked for extra tips. People all around were asking for tips for simple directions or just handouts. Mae was able to spend time with Mary again, and as a nurse, she would show concern for Mae's health and well-being. While in the Congo, Ronny stayed with her at all times for her own safety.

Mae's visit was longer this time, so she was able to see some of the other orphan children that she had not seen on her previous visit. She made an attempt to locate her other remaining orphans but was not able to. It was a bittersweet reunion, and although she was happy to see them, she was also saddened because her orphan children, along with the rest of the Congolese people, were still living in unacceptable conditions of poverty. It seemed that the dictator was plundering the country's wealth and pocketing it for his own personal gain. The country seemed to be going into bankruptcy during Mobutu's dictatorship. Everyone around Mobutu had money, but the common Congolese was poor. It seemed he had planned to be a dictator for life. It was said that he had been around sorcerers while practicing witchcraft and drinking human blood.

Mae didn't think it could get any worse from the last time she was in the Congo, but it looked like it had. During her visit to the Congo, the heat was blisteringly hot and dry. She was dehydrated from never having enough water to drink. Gary, one of the oldest of the children she had raised, was now a full-grown man with a family. He would bring food to her to make sure she had enough to eat. With the lack of resources and her frustration and disappointment, Mae realized that there was not much left she could do, and she needed to prepare to go back to the States. Her efforts would have to lie and remain there in the Congo.

She concluded her trip acknowledging that she would no longer have an orphanage in the Congo. She was hoping to regain the orphanage so the work there would continue in some capacity. She hoped that her children would continue where she had left off. Now, it seemed like not even a glimpse of hope was possible; Mae knew that she might be seeing her children in the Congo and saying goodbye to them for the last time. While on the airplane coming back to the United States, she reflected back on all the things she had experienced and all the people she had met and the difficult yet rewarding life she once had. Whatever time she had left, it would be lived out in the States.

Mae in her later years

Mae returned to their home in California and was able to spend time with her friends and family. Her close friend Erma, who everyone called Mawmaw Jackson, with whom she spent a lot of time through the years, passed away in August of 1986 at the age of ninety-two. Mae lived in the Claremont home until the last of her orphan children moved out. All of her adult children lived in close proximity to her, and the ones that didn't still made the effort to visit periodically.

Gaston would come around and fix up any repairs to the house or yard. He also cooked for Mae at times, as he did growing up in the orphanage. Bobby always helped out financially, supporting her. He did this from his high school days until Mae passed away. Bobby was also a strong spiritual encourager to her. Teddy would be there emotionally and physically to take her to her medical appointments, church, and to visit friends. Bobby, Teddy, and Ronny all had careers in law enforcement, while Gaston worked for a law firm. Gaston worked for a law firm.

Mae would spend the last few years of her life at a slower pace but still active. She always maintained her own personal morning and evening daily devotions. She enjoyed many activities in her later years, as health would permit. One activity was with a senior citizens group who made quilts for different causes. She also enjoyed touring on a senior bus, going to different cities within the state of California. Mae also enjoyed being taken by Teddy to the Trinity Broadcasting Studios, a Christian television network, to see different Christian ministers and singers from all denominations speak and perform.

Mae became a diabetic in the last few years of her life and was partially blind the last two years of her life. She sold her home and moved to a senior mobile home park with her two small dogs, Buffy and Peanut. She longed to see the Lord. She had run her race and fought the good fight. She was now ready to go to her permanent home in heaven. On January 19th, 1994, Mae went home to be with the Lord. She was eighty-three years of age, a month short of her eighty-fourth birthday.

Her children realized the injustice of everything that happened, and they vowed that they would do everything they could to see that their mother's legacy would continue in some aspect or another in the Congo. They knew that their mother wanted to continue the orphanage and that her heart would always lie in the Congo. They didn't know how it was going to happen, but they felt that God wanted them to continue their mother's legacy in some way or another.

CONCLUSION

In 1994, back in the Congo (Zaire), turmoil
erupted on its eastern border with Rwanda, which
spilled over into the country. Rwanda experienced
genocide of epic proportions. The conflict between
the Hutus and Tutsis would result in both parties
crossing borders into the Congo. The country
would also continue to decline, mainly due to
corruption and violence. In 1996, the rebel leader
Lauren Desire Kabila began defeating Congolese
soldiers on the eastern border and, by early 1997,
had marched his troops all the way through to the
edge of the capital city of Kinshasa. Kabila, who
wanted to avoid more bloodshed with President
Mobutu's soldiers, who were protecting Mobutu,
requested that he surrender peacefully. Mobutu, in
the face of obvious defeat, was willing to choose
bloodshed rather than relinquishing power.

Mobutu was reluctant to give up the title and
was willing to continue the civil war in order to
remain in power. It was at that time that Nelson
Mandela, president of South Africa, who was
highly respected around the world as a peacemaker,
came to Zaire (Congo) to intervene and set up

a meeting on May 4th, 1997, with Mobutu and Kabila. The intervention and meeting would result in Mobutu leaving the country in a peaceful manner without any bloodshed, and Mobutu would lose his title in the same way he had gained it: by way of a coup.

President Mobutu ruled for a total of thirty-two years, from 1965 to 1997. During that time, he plundered the country's many rich minerals. His self-worth is estimated at around four billion dollars. Meanwhile, the Congo, potentially one of the wealthiest countries in minerals and other natural resources, was plagued with corruption and economic ruin, leaving the average Congolese citizen living in poverty. Outside of World War I and World War II deaths, the Congo is said to have the most bloodshed on its land than any other country in the world in the twentieth century.

Mae lived in the Congo for a large part of that time, from 1946 to 1972. She faced a lot of uncertainty and adversity, but she faced it with faith. She lived a life of generosity, love, and service. She never gained anything for herself in terms of worldly gain, and in the end, she couldn't even hold on to the orphanage. But ultimately, she lived a life well-lived, in the service of others, especially loving and caring for children that no one else wanted.

APPENDIX

Timeline of the Kids in the Orphanage:

KIKWIT

1946— Christine (10), Louise (9), Joseph (8), Pierre (7), Mary (6)

IWUNGU

1949— David, Arline (infants)

MONGUNGU

1952— Timmy, Steven, Gaston (infants)

1953— Gary & Larry (twin infants), Ronny, Billy, Janette, Joanne, Lois, Mae-June (infants)

KINTSHUA

1954— Paul, Samuel (infants)

1956— Jack & Jaqueline (twin infants)

KALANDGANDA

1957— Gideon (4), Roland, Ruben, Martha (infants)

1958— Bobby (infant)

1959— Doris (infant), Joy (6), Dorothy (1 month)

1961— Dale, Betty, Yvonne (infants)

1962— Harold, Dick, Jimmy (infants)

1963— Wanda Lou (infant)

KINSHASA-KINTAMBO

1965— Teddy (2 weeks), Kay (2 months)

1966— Romaine (3), Ricky (infant), Marie (4), Marcaline (6)

1967— Nestor (5), Jean Pierre (5), Joshua (9)

1968— Evet (3), Sidone (10), Teresa (7)

1969— Lucisa (11), Kathalina (9)

KINSHASA-MACAMPAGNE

1970— Joseph (6)

1971— Ammina (4), Leo (4)

Fifty-four children's lives were touched through the orphanage.

ABOUT THE AUTHOR

Teddy Mubanza Clark was born in the Congo, Africa. He grew up and continues to reside in Southern California. He is now retired from a thirty-year career in law enforcement. He has been married to Evelyn for over seventeen years, who he met at Faith Church in West Covina, CA. They worked together as Sunday school teachers for young children, and Evelyn continues to serve in the children's ministry. He also served as the sports coordinator and now serves in security. Teddy continues to attend Faith Church, where he has been for over twenty-five years.

Teddy also volunteers at FCA (Fellowship of Christian Athletes) and has been an FCA board member in the LA County, San Gabriel Valley region, for over a decade. The ministry equips young men and women in junior high, high school, and college, and mentors them while sharing the Word of God. Teddy has also helped to mentor young students throughout his life, mainly through sports, while also sharing God's love and purpose for their lives.

Just like his mother, Teddy has a heart for children. He hopes that he, along with his brothers and sisters, can continue the legacy his mother started long ago in the Congo.

CPSIA information can be obtained
at www.ICGtesting.com
Printed in the USA
LVHW020412121022
730427LV00008B/53

9 781685 560386